The Origin of Philosophy

by JOSÉ ORTEGA Y GASSET

JOSÉ ORTEGA Y GASSET

THE ORIGIN OF PHILOSOPHY

AUTHORIZED TRANSLATION FROM THE SPANISH
BY TOBY TALBOT

W·W·NORTON & COMPANY·INC·New York

Library of Congress Catalog Card No. 67-12437

SBN 393 00128 8

Contents

Editors' Note

In 1943, during his residence in Lisbon, Ortega undertook the writing of an *Epilogue* to Julián Marías' *History of Philosophy*, originally published in 1941, and whose second edition was currently in preparation. Meanwhile the theme began to develop beyond its initial conception. On January 10, 1944, Ortega wrote to Marías: "The 'Epilogue' to your work will touch upon etymology and many other weighty topics. I have been engaged in it for months. Everything nowadays though, is so problematical, there are so many interferences to interrupt one's work, that I do not dare to venture great promises. But I do want you to know that I am up to my ears in your epilogue. I should like you however not to mention a word to anyone about it." Some months later, in June, Ortega announced to Marías that the epilogue would run to a 400-page volume, the most important of his books, and naturally would be published separately from the *History*, but with the title *Epilogue to Julián Marías' History of Philosophy*, all of which he wanted kept secret until the moment of its appearance. Toward the end of 1944, Ortega started giving a philosophy course in Lisbon, and on December 29 he again wrote to Marías: "The completed portion of the *Epilogue* will be included in it, and hopefully the *Epilogue* will derive mutual benefit, i.e., that its 700! pages will be published shortly."

In the summer of 1945, Ortega communicated to Marías his intention to detach a section from the *Epilogue* under the title *The Origin of Philosophy*. And in 1946, first in

Lisbon (*O Seculo*, April 13) and then in Madrid (ABC, April 26), he announced—keeping the secret—among his works in preparation, *Epilogue* . . . and *The Origin of Philosophy*. His arrival in Spain, various other commitments, the founding of the *Institute de Humanidades*, lengthy trips, and new works interrupted publication of the aforementioned writings, to which he always planned to return. In 1953 he published as an homage to Jaspers, under the title *Stücke aus einer "Geburt der Philosophie,"* a finished portion of *Origin of Philosophy* (in *Offener Horizont,* "Festschrift für Karl Jaspers zum 70. Geburtstag am 23. Februar 1953," R. Piper & Co., Verlag, Munich).

This entire volume provides an example of historic reason in operation on the central theme of the roots and historical justification of philosophy. One of the multiple tasks in which man has engaged is that of *making philosophy*, an occupation that has not been a permanent one for humanity, but as Ortega points out in this book, "came about one fine day in Greece and has indeed come down to us, with no guarantee, however, of its perpetuation." And he continues, "Without attempting now to formalize an opinion on this matter, I wish to suggest the possibility that what we are now beginning to engage in under the traditional aegis of philosophy is not another philosophy but something new and different from all philosophy."

Despite the fact that this work was never concluded, these writings constitute a decisive step in posing the problem of what philosophy is—its essential unity—in the same manner that historic reason is discovered through a retrospective contemplation of its total past and through the attempt to reconstruct the dramatic occasion of its origin.

Nihil invita Minerva
[Nothing with Minerva unwilling]

OLD LATIN SAYING, ACCORDING TO CICERO

The Origin of Philosophy

1
The Philosophical Past

AND NOW, WHAT? Julián Marías has presented us with an eventful film, the history of philosophy. He has performed his job admirably, rendering us in the process two lessons: one in the history of philosophy, and the other in sobriety, asceticism, and scrupulous commitment to a didactically inspired task. It would please me in this epilogue to avail myself of both these lessons, although with regard to the latter, I am unable to follow his example completely. Utmost sobriety was available to Marías since the doctrines expounded by him were existing doctrines, doctrines that had been previously developed and to which one could refer in various texts. An *epilogue*, however, is something that follows a logos—in this instance, philosophical doctrines or "statements." Hence, it consists in the things one can say about things that have already been said—constituting thereby a futuristic statement, a heretofore nonexistent one, and thus we can hardly refer to it in ampler, pre-existent texts. This task I have undertaken at Marías' behest. Having committed myself, I shall endeavor to perform it with a measure of brevity, and if possible, with the clarity demanded by the intent of this book.

A statement is a kind of act, or doing. What is a reader *to do* upon concluding a history of philosophy? Caprice is to be avoided. Caprice signifies doing anything among the many things that can be done. Its opposite is the act and habit of *choosing* from among many things precisely the one that demands to be done. This act and habit of choosing selectively was at first designated as *eligentia* by the Latins, and then *elegantia*. This term is possibly the origin of our word *int-elligencia*. In any event, *elegance* would have been an apter name for what we instead awkwardly categorize as ethics; since the latter is the art of choosing the best conduct, it is the science of what has to be done. The fact that the term *elegance* is nowadays a most irritating one is its highest recommendation. Elegant is the man who neither does nor says any old thing, but instead does what should be done and says what should be said.

There is nothing equivocal about what one is to do after he finishes reading a history of philosophy. It is automatically presented to us. The first thing is to cast a final retrospective gaze at the sweeping avenue of philosophical doctrines. The past comes to an end in the final chapter of Marías' text, but we, the readers, must continue. We do not remain upon the shore of the continent on which we now stand. To remain in the past means to be dead. With the final glance of travelers pursuing their inexorable destiny, the search for green pastures, we sum up the past, evaluate it, and take leave of it. Bound for where? The past borders on the future, for the present, which theoretically separates them, is such a tenuous line that it merely serves to join and unite them. The present, at least in man, is a vessel with fragile walls, filled almost to the brim with memories and expectations. In fact, one could practically say that the present is a mere pretext for the existence of the past and of the future, the juncture where both derive meaning.

A retrospective glance, in which we cull the essence of the philosophical past, provides the realization that, though we might desire to do so, it is impossible to remain there. Not one "philosophical system" among those formulated appears adequately true to us. Anyone who pre-

sumes to be able to settle into some bygone doctrine—
and I refer, of course, only to someone fully conscious
of what he is doing—is suffering an optical illusion. At
best, anyone who adopts a philosophy of the past does
not leave it intact, but must, in order to adopt it, remove
and add to it no small number of pieces, in view of subsequent philosophies.

Hence a final backward gaze invariably incites in us
an alternate forward one. Unable to find lodging among
the philosophies of the past, we have no choice but to
attempt to construct one of our own. The history of the
philosophical past catapults us into the still empty spaces
of the future, toward a philosophy yet to come. This
epilogue can merely serve to give expression, albeit elementary and speculative, to some of the multitudinous
things encompassed by both of these gazes. To my mind,
at the present juncture, that is what demands to be said.

By the end of a history of philosophy, the reader has
had a complete panoramic view of the philosophical past
presented to him. This view initiates in any reader—providing he has not bogged down in the process but has
retained his inner bearings—a dialectical series of thoughts.

Thoughts can be linked with evidence in two ways.
By the first, a thought appears as though emerging from
a previous one because it is simply an expansion of something implicit in the first. Whereupon we say that the
first thought *implied* the second. This is analytic thought:
a series of thoughts develops from an initial thought by
virtue of progressive analysis.

There is, however, another manner of connection evident between ideas. Should we desire to think of the
body of the Earth, we think of a nearly round object
of a given size, slightly depressed around both polar
regions, and according to recent findings, likewise a bit
depressed in the equatorial zone—in short, a spheroid.

This alone, then, is what we are interested in thinking about. It turns out, however, that we are unable to think of this in isolation, for upon thinking of this, we juxtapose, or simultaneously think about, the space around the spheroid, a space that confines or situates it. This addition was unforeseen and unintentional. Yet in actuality we have no alternative; *if* we think of the spheroid, we think also of the space around it. Now it is evident that the concept of the "surrounding space" was not included or implied in the concept "spheroid." Nevertheless, the first idea irresistibly imposes upon us the second, lest the former remain incomplete, and likewise our thinking on it. The concept "spheroid" does not implicate, it *complicates* the concept "surrounding space." This process is synthetic or dialectic thought.[1]

In a dialectical series of thoughts, each thought presents a complication and impels one on to the next thought. The connection between them is thus much stronger than in analytic thought. By the latter method we *may* think about the concept implied in the antecedent, and once it is thought about, we are compelled to recognize their mutual "identification," although there was no obligation to think about it. The first concept wants for naught; it is serene and seemingly self-contained. In synthetic thought,

1. Philosophy of course has always practiced synthetic thought, though prior to Kant no one had focused upon its peculiarity. Kant "discovered" it and named it, contemplating, however, only its negative aspect, namely, that it was not analytic thought or implication. And since, in philosophic tradition—particularly the immediate one, that is, Leibnitz—implication appeared to be the only evident connection between two ideas, he believed that synthetic thought was not evident. His successors—Fichte, Schelling, Hegel—took into account the role of evidence, but still remained unaware of its origin and mode of operation. Husserl, who barely discussed synthetic thought, was most responsible for clarifying its nature. Nonetheless, we are still on the threshold of the task of mastering it, and much remains yet to be done, as will be suggested subsequently in this epilogue.

however, not only may we, but we must, *velis nolis*, juxtapose another concept. We might say in this instance that evidence of the connection between two concepts exists prior to any thought on the second, for it is that which impels us to the second. The dialectic is the obligation to continue thinking, and this is not merely a manner of speaking, but an actual reality. It is the very fact of the human condition. Man genuinely has no recourse but to "continue thinking," for he always discovers that he has not thought anything out completely, but must integrate it with what has already been thought, or else recognize that he might just as well not have thought at all, and consequently feel lost.

This major fact does not clash with another minor one, namely that each of us, *de facto,* halts, is arrested, and ceases to think at a given point in a dialectical series. Some stop sooner than others. This, however, does not mean that we did not *have to* continue thinking. Although we stop, the dialectical series continues, and the need to pursue it is incumbent upon us. But other pressures in life, illness, or simply differing capacities to pursue undeviatingly and lucidly a lengthy chain of ideas account for our *violent* interruption of the dialectic series. We cut it short, but it continues to bleed within us. The brute fact of having suspended it does not signify failure to realize the obvious urgency to pursue our thinking. A somewhat analogous process occurs in chess: a player feels incapable of anticipating, without getting utterly confused, two possible plays, each of an equal number of moves and each emerging from a given position of the pieces on the board. Having decided to suspend anticipation of further moves, he does not remain at peace; on the contrary, he foresees the imminent threat of checkmate. Yet, he is incapable of greater effort.

Let us endeavor, then, to retrace in its principal phases

the dialectical series of ideas automatically released in us by a retrospective view of the philosophical past. Our first impression is that of a multitude of opinions on the same subject; in the nature of multitudes, some opinions contradict others, and by their contradiction they are mutually incriminatory of error. The philosophical past thus strikes us at first glance as a congeries of errors. When the Greeks paused in their creative trajectory of doctrines to cast their first retrospective glance of pure historical contemplation,[2] that too was their initial impression, and by stopping there, by not continuing their thinking, skepticism was born. Hence Agrippa's famous *trope* or argument against the possibility of attaining truth: the "dissonance of opinions"—*diafonia ton doxon*. Systems appear as aborted attempts to construct the edifice of truth. Thence the past is viewed as error. Hegel, referring more generally to all of human life, maintained that "when turning our gaze to the past the first thing we observe is ruins." Ruin, in fact, is the countenance of the past.

Noteworthy is the fact that we are not the ones to discover the breach of error in bygone doctrines, for a reading of history reveals how each new philosophy began with a denunciation of its predecessor, and further, that by its formal recognition of the latter's invalidity, it identified itself as another philosophy.[3] Hence the his-

2. Aristotle continually reviews earlier doctrines, not from an historical viewpoint, but as if they were contemporary opinions that must be taken into account. Historical perspective perhaps is evinced in Aristotle only in his reference to certain philosophers as "the ancients"—*hoi palaioi*—and his observation that they are still amateurs—*apeiria*.

3. One fact that ought to be more startling to us than it ordinarily is, is that once the profession of philosophy exists formally, no philosophy appears to begin anew, but all emerge from their predecessors, and—after a certain point—one can say, from all prior ones. Nothing seemingly would be more "natural" in the history of philosophy than if now and then some appeared that bore no precedent to others, but that were spontaneous and *a nihilo*. But

tory of philosophy is simultaneously an exposition of systems and, unintentionally, a critique of them. It represents an effort to construct doctrine after doctrine, though
once each is constructed it is beheaded by its successor,
and time is strewn with corpses. Thus it is not merely
the abstract fact of "dissonance" that makes us view the
past as error, but in a manner of speaking, it is the past
itself that is daily committing suicide, discrediting itself,
bringing ruin upon itself. One can seek no refuge in it.
This awesome experience of failure is perfectly expressed
in the following passage by Bossuet—an outstanding example, by the way, of the baroque style, the manner in
which Western man expressed himself in every order of
life between 1550 and 1700: "When I reflect upon this
turbulent sea, if I may rightly thus refer to human opinion and reasoning, I find it impossible in so vast a realm
to come upon any secure shelter or tranquil retreat that
has not been memorialized already by the shipwreck of
some celebrated navigator."[4]

In the dialectical series, then, this is the *first thought:*
The history of philosophy *prima facie* reveals the past
to us as a defunct world of errors.

SECOND THOUGHT

We have not, however, thought the first one through
"completely." We said earlier that each philosophy sets
out by revealing the errors of its predecessor or predecessors and that in so doing it is another philosophy. This
would be senseless if each philosophy were not formally,
in some dimension, an effort to eliminate preceding errors

this has never happened, whereas the reverse has, to a great extent.
This bears emphasis, particularly in relation to our present comments on the force of the dialectical process and to other statements that will follow regarding philosophy as tradition.

4. *Sermon on the Law of God, for Quincuagesma Sunday.*

—which provides us with a sudden illumination and discloses a second aspect of the past. We continue to see it as consistently committing errors, but now the errors, despite their nature and precisely because of it, are transformed into involuntary instruments of the truth. In its initial aspect, error possessed a purely negative dimension, whereas by its second aspect, errors as such acquire a positive facet. Each philosophy profits from the mistakes of previous ones and is born, secure *a limine* that it, at least, will not fall prey to those same errors. And so on successively. The history of philosophy can now be likened to a scalded cat fleeing the house in which it was burned. In this manner, as time moves on, philosophy accumulates in its saddle bag a collection of recognized errors, which *ipso facto* are transformed into truth-seeking aids. The shipwrecks that Bossuet spoke about are perpetuated in the guise of buoys and beacons that provide warning of reefs and sand bars. In this second aspect, therefore, the past appears to us as an arsenal and a treasury of errors.

THIRD THOUGHT

We are currently accustomed to regard truth as something quite unattainable. This attitude is reasonable. Simultaneously, however, we are prone to think of error as being overly likely, which is less salutary. Paradoxically, contemporary man confronts the existence of error lightly. That error exists seems the most "natural" thing in the world to him. He does not question its existence. He accepts it without further ado, to the extent that when reading the history of philosophy he is taken aback by the Greeks' tenacious efforts to explain the possibility of error. One might say that this habituation to the existence of error, as to a domestic object, is the same thing as contemporary man's innate skepticism. I fear, however, that such a statement may in turn be equally frivolous, and, indeed, indicative of megalomania. Anything is called skepticism! As if skepticism could be an innate state of mind, or bestowed upon someone with no prior effort on his part! The blame for this rests upon that force, both delightful and repellent, mighty and base, known as language. The existence of language is, in a way, a continual denigration of words. This denigration, like almost everything in language, is produced mechanically, that is, senselessly. Language is a usage. Usage is the social fact par excellence, and society is, not accidentally, but in its most radical essence, senseless. It is everything human dehumanized, "despiritualized," and transformed into a mere mechanism.[5] The word "skepticism" is a technical term coined in Greece at the summit of Greek intelligence. It designated certain dreadful men who denied the possibility of truth, a primordial and basic illusion of man. Hence, it does not refer simply to people who "did not believe in anything." At all times and in all places numerous men have existed who "did not believe in anything," precisely because "they did not question anything"; living, for them, meant simply abandoning oneself from one moment to the next, without any inner response or position in the face of any dilemma. Believing in something assumes an active nonbelieving in other things, which in turn implies having questioned many things, in opposition to which others seemed "unquestionable," hence our be-

5. The first time I publicly expounded this notion of society, the basis of a new sociology, was at a lecture delivered in Valladolid in 1934, under the title "Man and People." Innumerable events have hitherto prevented me from publishing the book which, under that same title, should develop my entire social doctrine. [*El hombre y la gente*, (Madrid, Editorial Revista de Occidente, 1957). Translated in English as *Man and People* (New York, W. W. Norton & Co., Inc., 1963).]

lief in them. This explains why I speak in quotes about the sort of person who now exists and always has—the individual who "doesn't believe in anything." I wish thereby to indicate the inadequacy of so qualifying his state of mind, inasmuch as genuine nonbelief does not occur in him. Such an individual neither believes nor fails to believe. He is outside of all such matters; he does not "engage" reality or nothingness. He exists in a lifelong state of somnolence. Things neither exist nor nonexist for him and therefore he does not feel the brunt of either belief or disbelief in them.[6] This temperament of stupor toward life is nowadays classified as "skepticism" through a debasement of the word. A Greek would be unable to understand this current use of the word, for the designation "sceptics"—*skepticoi*—for him, applied to terrifying men. Terrifying not because they "didn't believe in anything"—that was their business!—but because they would not allow one to live; they descended upon one and uprooted one's belief in the things that seemed most true, instilling in one's head, as though with gleaming surgical instruments, a series of tight, rigorous, inescapable arguments. All of which implied that those men had previously performed upon their own living flesh, without anesthetic, the same operation—they had conscientiously made themselves "nonbelievers." And even prior to engaging in this, they had stubbornly driven themselves to create the sharp instruments, those "arguments against the truth" that they employed in their task of amputation. The word reveals the Greek view of the skeptic: a figure diametrically opposed to the somnolent type of individual who

6. Man, of course, always stands amid countless elemental beliefs, the major portion of which he is unaware. With respect to this, see my study *Ideas y Creencias* [*Ideas and Beliefs*, Vol. V]. The theme of nonbelief, which the above text touches upon, is discussed on the level of patent human affairs, upon which men speak and argue.

abandons himself and allows himself to be carried along by life. They called him an "investigator," but since this term, too, has deteriorated in form, let us say, to be more exact, that they called him a "seeker." The philosopher at that early date was a man of extraordinary mental and moral energy. The skeptic, however, was even more so, for whereas the former exhausted himself in the quest for the truth, the latter was not content with that alone; he went further, he continued thinking and analyzing the truth until it was proven invalid. Thus, along with the basic meaning of "seeker," the Greek word has traces of such connotations as "hyperactive person," "heroic," and to a considerable degree, "sinister hero," "indefatigable," and hence, "fatiguing," someone with whom one "can do nothing." He was the human drill. Note that the term "skeptic" only later became a classification for a philosophical school, a doctrine—the first semantic debasement of the term.[7] Originally it signified the vocational,

7. The reason for this: One who is a skeptic in accordance with some mode, *because* he belongs to a school, is such as a recipient, and not as a result of his own creation; hence he is a "secondary," habitualized skeptic, or to some extent deficient and inauthentic. Likewise, and for similar though not identical reasons, the word is gradually losing significant vigor. Traditional linguistics recognizes the phenomena in its most external manifestation and speaks of *strong* and *weak* words, and even with respect to a word of the varying degree of strength, weakness, "emptiness" (Chinese grammar), etc., in its meaning. Clearly, however, if language on the one hand represents a degeneration of words, it must necessarily constitute in addition a marvelous generative force. A word suddenly becomes *charged* with a meaning that it *conveys to us* with a plasticity, relief, clarity, suggestiveness, or, one may deign to call it, a superlative force. Without any effort on our part to vitalize its meaning, it *discharges* its semantic *charge* upon us like a spark of electricity. I call this "the word in due form," which acts as an incessant revelation. It is perfectly feasible to go through the dictionary and take the pulse of semantic energy of each word at a given date. The classic comparison of words with currency is legitimate and fruitful. The reason for their similarity is identical: usage. Linguists could profitably inquire into this topic. Not only

incoercible calling of certain particular individuals, a heretofore unheard of and never practiced profession, and hence one without an established name, one that had to be named by what they were seen doing: seeking or "scrutinizing" truths, that is, subjecting truths to further scrutiny than other people, questioning things beyond the point where philosophers believe that through their effort they are unquestionable.

Clearly, then, the true skeptic, unlike contemporary man, is not inherently endowed with his skepticism. His doubt is not a "state of mind," but something acquired, the result of a process as laborious as the most compressed dogmatic philosophy.

In the generations before our own—let us not at the moment pinpoint exactly when or why—a decline occurred in what Plato called the "quest for Being," or for truth. Although there has existed a vast and fertile curiosity—hence the expansion and exquisite refinement in the sciences—a surging impulse toward clarification on fundamental problems is now notably lacking. One of these problems is that of truth and its correlate, authentic Reality. The aforementioned generations luxuriated in the progressive miracle of the natural sciences, which terminate in techniques. They allowed themselves to be transported by train and automobile. Note, however, in passing, that since 1880 Western man has not possessed one governing philosophy. Positivism was the last. Since then only a particular individual, or a particular limited social group, are possessors of a philosophy. Indubitably

---

would they disclose many interesting facts—these they already possess—but also some new and heretofore undisclosed linguistic categories. For some time—despite the fact that I know next to nothing about linguistics—I have attempted, tangentially, to remark upon the accomplishments and shortcomings of language; for although I am not a linguist, I have certain things to say that perhaps are not utterly trivial.

since 1800 philosophy has progressively ceased to be a component of general culture and hence a present historical factor. Never before in Europe's history has this happened.

Only the individual who is in a position to question things with precision and urgency—whether they definitely exist or not—is able to experience genuine belief and disbelief. This same *asthenia* in attacking the problem of truth is what also prevents us from viewing error as a formidable problem. The impossibility of an absolute error need merely be suggested. So inconceivable is the latter that it thrusts us headlong into another dreadful enigma: senselessness. The problems of error and of dementia are mutually intertwined.

In its second aspect, the philosophical past appears as an arsenal and treasury of errors, but with that in mind we must realize that we have carried our thinking about the concept of the "precious error," the error transmuted into positive and fertile magnitude, only half-way.

It is impossible for a philosophy to be an absolute error. The error must contain some element of truth. Moreover, it was proven an error as the result of detection, since at the outset it was believed to be a truth. This makes it evident that it contained no small measure of truth if it was able to substitute for it so well. And if we analyze more closely the nature of the "refutation"—as they say in the seminaries employing this ghastly term—that one philosophy exerts upon its predecessor, it is apparent that the process is not at all similar to an electrocution, although the phonetics of the word would seem to promise no less awesome a spectacle. In the final analysis it is revealed to be an error not because it was untrue, but because it was not true enough. The earlier philosopher stopped prematurely in the dialectical series of his thoughts; he did not "continue thinking." The fact is that his successor utilizes the former doctrine, incorporates it into his new repertory of ideas, and simply avoids the mistake of stopping there. The process is clear: The earlier philosopher exerted himself to reach a particular point—like the aforementioned struggling chess player—whereas his successor, without any exertion, *receives* the accomplished labor, apprehends it, and by applying fresh vigor, is able to employ it as a point of departure and advance still further. In the new system, the received thesis does not remain exactly as it was in the old; it is completed. Thus it is actually a new and different idea from the original criticized and subsequently incorporated one. Let us recognize that the defective idea, convicted of error, *disappears* within the new intellectual creation. It disappears because it is assimilated into another more complete one. This adventure of ideas that die, not through annihilation, leaving no trace, but because they are *surpassed* by other more complex ones, is what Hegel called *Aufhebung*, a term I translate as "absorption." The absorbed element disappears *into* the absorber and thereby is simultaneously abolished and preserved.[8]

This brings us to a third aspect of the philosophical past. The aspect of error as it *prima facie* appears to us turns out to be a mask. Now the mask has been removed and we view errors as incomplete partial truths, or as is usually said, "they are partially true," hence, portions of truth. You might say that before men began to think, reason was broken into bits, and thereafter men had to go about picking up the pieces one by one and putting them together. Simmel talks about a "broken-plate society"

8. "Absorption" is such an evident and repeated phenomenon that it leaves no room open for doubt. In Hegel, however, it is in addition an integral thesis of his entire system, and as such is unrelated to the foregoing statements. Likewise, the Hegelian dialectic should not be thought of in connection with my foregoing and future discussion of the "dialectical series."

that existed in Germany at the end of the last century. Some friends at the conclusion of a commemorative dinner decided to break a plate and to divide the pieces, each one agreeing to surrender his piece to one of his friends upon his death. In this manner the fragments gradually fell into the hands of the last survivor, who was able to reconstruct the plate.

Those insufficient or partial truths are experiences in thought that, with respect to Reality, must be undergone. Each of them is a "path" or "road"—*methodos*—whereby a segment of the truth is traversed and one of its aspects contemplated. A point is reached, however, where one can pursue *that path* no further. It is obligatory to try a different one. For that—for it to be different—one must bear its predecessor in mind; in this sense, it is a continuation of the former, but with a change of direction. If previous philosophers had not undergone those "experiences in thought," the successors would have had to undergo them, and hence, would themselves remain at that point and be, as it were, the predecessor. From this viewpoint, the succession of philosophers appears as one single philosopher who lived for twenty-five hundred years during which he "continued thinking." According to this third aspect, the philosophical *past* is revealed to us as a vast melody of intellectual experiences through which man has been *passing*.

FOURTH THOUGHT

The philosopher who lived for twenty-five hundred years can be said to exist; he is the present-day philosopher. In our present philosophical conduct and in the doctrine produced thereby, we view and take into consideration a substantial portion of previous thought on themes relating to our discipline. This is tantamount to declaring that past philosophies are our collaborators, that they persist and survive in our own philosophy.

When we first comprehend philosophy, we are struck by the truth it contains and reflects—that is, were we for the moment unfamiliar with other philosophies, it would strike us then and there as the very truth. Hence the study of each philosophy, even for someone expert in such encounters, is an unforgettable illumination. Subsequent consideration leads to rectification: such and such a philosophy is not valid, but another is. This nonetheless does not nullify and invalidate the first impression; the archaic doctrine remains true "for the moment"—understanding truth to be something that takes place in the mental itinerary toward a more complete one. The latter arrival is more complete because it includes, it absorbs, the former.

Each philosophy contains elements of the others, like the necessary steps in a dialectical series. The presence of these elements will be evident to a greater or lesser degree, and possibly an entire older system will appear in the more modern one in the guise of merely a stump or rudiment. This is patently and incontestably so, if a past philosophy is compared with its predecessors. Moreover, the reverse also obtains: If a prior philosophy is examined, one can discern in vague outline, and still incomplete embodiment, the germs of many subsequent ideas—if one takes into account the degree of explicitness, richness, dimension, and distinction typical of the times when the antiquated philosophy was conceived. This can not help being so. Since the problems of philosophy are radical problems, there is no philosophy that does not contain them all. The radical problems are inexorably linked to one another and departure from any one leads to the other. The philosopher always sees them, though possibly not clearly, consciously, and connectedly. If one feels that this cannot properly be called seeing, one may call it blindly sensing. Hence, contrary to what the layman believes, all philosophies have a very good mutual understanding of one another: they constitute a conversation that has lasted for nearly three milleniums, a perpetual dialogue and dispute held in a common tongue, namely the philosophical viewpoint itself and the perennial existence of the same difficult problems.

This brings us to a *fourth aspect* of the philosophical past. The previous aspect allowed us to regard the melody of intellectual experiences through which man must pass in confronting certain themes. The past was thus provided with an affirmation, a justification. It remained, however, where it was—in the realm of what has been. Embalmed, but finally dead. It was an archeological view. Now, however, we realize that those formed experiences must be continually reconstructed, albeit with the benefit of having been received ready-made. Thus we do not leave them behind, but our present philosophy is in great part the current resuscitation of all the yesterdays of philosophy. The efficacy of old ideas is perpetually restored in us and becomes everlasting. Instead of imagining the philosophical past as a line stretched horizontally in time, the new aspect compels us to imagine it as a vertical line, because the past continues to operate, weighing upon us and upon the present. Our philosophy is what it is because it finds itself mounted upon the shoulders of its predecessors—like "the human tower" number performed in the circus by a family of acrobats. Or, if you prefer another image, one can view philosophizing humanity as a long, long road that must be traversed century after century, but a road that in the process winds upon itself, and becomes a load on the traveler's back—it is transformed from a road into luggage.

This process of the philosophical past is simply one

example of what happens with all the human past.

The historical past is not past simply because it is not now in the present—that would be an extrinsic characterization—but because *it has passed* or happened to other men whom we remember, and consequently it *keeps happening* to us in our continual repassing or reviewing of it.*

Man is the only being who is a product of the past, who consists in the past, though not solely in the *past*. Other things do not *possess* it because they are only a consequence of the past: cause and effect are left behind; the past is obliterated. Man, however, preserves it within himself, he accumulates it, he enables that which once was to subsist within "in the form of what has been."9 This possession of the past, its preservation (the quality that is most specifically human is not so-called intellect, but "felicitous memory"),10 is equivalent to a modest attempt, but an attempt, nevertheless, at eternity—thus do we resemble, to some small degree, God; for possession of the past in the present is one of the characteristics of eternity. If, in like sense, we also *possessed* the future, our lives would be a total imitation of eternity—as Plato held, with much less cause, with respect to time itself. The future, though, is precisely what is problematic, unsure, that which can or cannot be; we do not *possess* it except in the measure in which we predict it. Hence man's perpetual urge to divine, to prophesy. In modern times a great step forward has been made in the ability

* *Pasado* (the past) in Spanish finds its counterpart in the verb *pasar* (to happen) and *repasar* (to review), making the entire concept linguistically compact.—*Trans.*

9. Regarding this category of historical reason, which is "being in the form of having been," see my study *History as a System* [*Complete Works*, Vol. VI].

10. See my *Prologue* to the Count of Yebes book [*Complete Works*, Vol. VI].

to predict: natural science rigorously predicts many future events. It is curious to note that the Greeks did not qualify as knowledge *sensu stricto* an intellectual method such as our physical science which, according to them, is content with "keeping up appearances"—Τὰ Φαινόμενα σῴζειν—but they did end up calling it an "ingenious devination." Consult Cicero's treatise *De Divinatione* for a definition of the latter, taken probably from Posidonius, and say whether it is not the definition of physical science.[11]

Man is able to predict more and more of the future, and hence "eternalize" himself more in that dimension. Meanwhile, he has also attained greater possession of his past. When the present conflicts come to an end, man will probably engage in assimilating the past with unparalleled zeal and urgency, and display astounding scope, vigor, and accuracy. I call this phenomenon, which I have anticipated for years, *the dawn of historical reason.*

Man is thus now on the brink of increasing his measure of "eternity." For being eternal does not mean enduring, or having existed in the past, existing in the present, and continuing to exist in the future. That is simply self-perpetuation, everlasting being—a task that is, finally, fatiguing, since it signifies that one has had to span *all* of time. Self-eternalization however is the opposite; it means not moving from the present, but allowing the past and future to attain the present and occupy it; it signifies remembering and foreseeing. In a sense it accomplishes with time what Belmonte accomplished with bulls; instead of maneuvering around the bull he succeeded in getting the bull to maneuver around him. The pity is that the bull of Time, insofar as one can concretely presume,

11. *De Divinatione* i, XLIX (I quote from the Didot edition because I have none other at my disposal). The term "ingenious divination," I believe, does not appear until I, LVI.

always ends up horning the man who strives to become eternal.

Man's "eternity," even that which is actually possible, is only probable. Man must always tell himself what the fifteenth-century Burgundian gentleman chose as a motto: *Rien ne m'est sûr que la chose incertain*—the only thing I am certain of is uncertainty. No one has assured us that the scientific spirit will persist in mankind, and the evolution of science is ever threatened by involution, retrogression, and even vanishment.

This retrospection of ours makes it evident that *it is a matter of indifference whether the philosophical past is designed as an accumulation of errors or an accumulation of truths*, because in fact it contains elements of both. Each of the two judgments is partial, and instead of fighting each other, it is to the advantage of each to unite and join hands. The dialectical series we have pursued is not, in its thematic points, a chain of arbitrary thoughts that are justifiable only on a personal basis, but they constitute the mental itinerary anyone must pursue who sets out to reflect upon the reality: "the philosophical past." It is not arbitrary, nor are we responsible for the fact that in departing from its totality, the first thing that is noticed is the multitude of contradictory opinions—and hence erroneous ones—whereupon we realize how each philosophy evades the mistake incurred by its precursor and thus profits from it. We thereupon realize that this would be impossible if said mistake were not partially true, and finally, that those portions of truth are integrated by being resuscitated in contemporary philosophy. Just as a physicist finds that in a normal experiment things happen in a determined way, that repetition in a modern laboratory produces the same result, so a thinker finds that a series of mental steps are imposed upon him. His concentration or detainment at particular junctures may vary, but all are stations at which his intellect will *pause* momentarily. As we shall see, the function of intellect is *to pause*, and therefore to detain the reality that confronts man. In the process of following the series, the time expended will vary depending upon one's abilities, physical bent, climatic conditions, and state of repose or disquiet.[12] The adroit mind generally covers an elementary dialectical series, such as the one here expounded, with utmost speed. This skill is born of training, and is neither more nor less mysterious than gymnastics or "memory training." Anyone can be a philosopher if he wants to—assuming he is willing to make the effort, and in fact, wealth acts almost as a greater detriment than poverty.[13] With the realization that the philosophical past *is*, *in reality*, *indifferent* to its aspect of error and to its aspect of truth, we ought in our behavior to *abandon* neither, but to *integrate* both.

A truth, if it is not complete, is something with which one cannot remain—where one cannot stay or stand. Recall the initial example of the spheroid and the space around it. No sooner does one dwell upon the former

12. I shall utilize this occasion to insert a pedagogical interpolation directed to inexperienced young individuals—young signifying that one is professionally inexperienced. It is very likely that such a reader may react to my foregoing statements in the following way: "This is all self-evident and trivial. We all know that every day is not the same. Therefore, the writer in saying this and in heaping up expressions that amount to the same thing—that is, 'how one feels'—is indulging in 'rhetoric.' In any event, none of this represents a philosophical problem." To which I must reply that when he reaches p . . . (indication that the page is blank in the manuscript, and that apparently the author never got to write it) let him recall this reaction of his, for he will thereupon receive a *choc* that is extremely useful in learning how to read philosophical texts.

13. Cf. my essay *Man and Crisis*, concerning how wealth and the superabundance of possessions are the causes of great and sometimes horrendous historical crises [*Complete Works*, Vol. V].

than he is forced into thinking about the "space around
it." Hence, the common expression "X stands mistaken"
has great intrinsic meaning, if we care to note it. Implicit
in it is the suggestion that error is precisely "a state where
one cannot stand."[14] If one could *stand* mistaken there
would be no sense in pursuing the truth. And in fact our
language employs another related expression, which reveals something implicit in the former one: "X has fallen
into the same mistake as . . . " Hence, being mistaken
means falling—the very opposite of "standing." In other
instances this problematical "standing" in error is given
a bias, always a negative and moral one; not only does it
represent a fall but "an error is committed . . . ," thereby
placing the responsibility for the fall upon the one who
has fallen.

Since past truths[15] are incomplete one cannot stand or
rest on them, and *for that reason* alone, they are errors.
If there are errors of another sort—that is, errors that are
simply errors, whose error does not consist sheerly in
their fragmentary nature but in their content and substance—that is a topic which at present need not be elab-
orated. Let us interrupt this dialectical series not because,
strictly speaking, it ought not to be pursued, but because
the occasion of this epilogue does not allow for further

14. To clarify: Inherent in this expression is a reprobative intention. X does something that for one reason or other cannot be
done—he stands mistaken. This pertains to a class of expressions
such as—X is a traitor, Y tells lies, Z confuses things—which,
though affirmative gramatically, state negative concepts. The negation is stated in the predicate, which is also affirmative in gram-
matical form, although the speaker clearly and admittedly
recognizes that it unquestionably constitutes a negative reality.

15. To speak about "past truth" seemingly indicates that truth
has a date attached to it, that it dates, whereas truth has always
been defined as something apart from time. We shall subsequently
explore this further, but for the present I merely wish to advise the
reader that this is not a verbal *lapsus* and that if it is a crime it is
not unpremeditated.

elaboration, and enough has been said already. According to the foregoing, however, is error not the interruption of a dialectical series, the failure to "continue thinking"? This would be true, were we to consider the foregoing as complete; but what we are doing is simply deciding that it is adequate for the present scope and pertinence of our subject. Obviously everything in the preceding series, as well as in our initial backward glance, was simply an attempt at a broad macrocosm. Clearly, countless things remain to be said in the direction of that thought. In addition to which, the foregoing statements are elementary—and elementary things are invariably the most crude and gross, though they must be stated and cannot justifiably be omitted.[16]

16. Neither my allotted space nor the didactic aim of this book permit me to expand more freely on this subject. As I speak, I can imagine some readers who are not too skilled yet in the ways of philosophy. To facilitate their task I have provided this first dialectical series with a form and even a certain typographical relief that underscores the stages of thought as it advances in its progressive complication or synthesis. In the remaining pages I shall abandon such a procedure in order to progress more rapidly, tacitly assuming that the reader will understand and provide many of the intermediary *steps*.

Whenever possible, however, it is desirable to spare readers the demoralizing annoyance resulting from intimations that certain things of greater interest and substance have remained unformulated, failing to provide the reader with any concrete notion of what is being withheld. Since this, in turn, is impractical in most instances, without incurring a hermetic manner of expression— one compounded of laconism and technicality—only now and then and by way of example is there space to enumerate specific topics that were not touched upon. The reader thereby gains confidence in a writer, trusts him, and is convinced that intimations of latent profundities and postponed rigorisms are actualities. In short, it is to the advantage of both reader and author that the latter's silence not be open to misinterpretation, or to the accusation of vacuousness, but that it be even clearer than the things he says.

With this in mind I am herewith enumerating a few of the many topics that the series begun in this chapter would eventually encounter were it to continue. I shall mention those that lend

On the other hand, after a brief reflection on what we have just done, which will yield us an important ontological theorem, we are going to begin another dialectical series whose point of departure will be the same (the philosophic past) but whose route will be different.

---

themselves to brief statement and can be understood without special preparation and are, moreover, open problems, the solution of which would demand lengthy investigations, even of an empirical nature, with facts and "data."

1. Before philosophy began, what analagous profession existed among men? If philosophy is, in its turn, merely one step taken by thought upon the heels of another, which would not be philosophy, this means that all of philosophy, from its onset to the present, would appear as merely one member of a "dialectical" series of much greater breadth than it is. I shall have more to say on this inomissible subject further on.

2. Why did philosophy begin, and when and where did it begin?

3. Did this beginning, by its concrete circumstance, ballast philosophy with millenary limitations from which it must free itself?

4. Why in each period does philosophy stop at a particular point?

5. Have certain experiences been absent from the melody of intellectual experiences comprised by the philosophical past? This for me would be of particular significance insofar as the reader would then realize that the statements in this text do not presuppose the historical process of philosophy to be "the way it should have been," that it is free from imperfections, gaps, serious defects, important omissions, etc. According to Hegel, the historical process—the human one in general and the philosophical one specifically—has been perfect, that which it "had to be," that which "it should have been." History, he maintains, is "rational"— though one clearly understands that this "rationality" (which he believes history to possess) is not historical "reason," but with slight modification, is the kind familiar since the days of Aristotle and recognizable ever since as the opposite of historicity—the invariable, the "eternal." In my opinion, it is imperative to invert Hegel's formula and maintain that rather than history being "rational," the fact is that reason, authentic reason, is historical. The traditional concept of reason is abstract, imprecise, utopian, and unchronological. But since everything that exists must be concrete *if reason exists*, it will have to be "concrete reason." See this author's *History as a System* [1935] and his early formu-

lations of the idea, *The Modern Theme* [1923]. Something on the
historicity of reason appears in *Being in One's Self and Being
Beside One's Self* [Buenos Aires, 1939] and in my Prologue to
Veinte Años de Caza Mayor by the Count of Yebes [1943]
(*Complete Works*, Vols. II, III, V, and VI). The essay *Being in
One's Self and Being Beside One's Self* forms Chapter I of *Man
and People.*

2
Aspects and the Entirety

IF FOR THE TIME BEING we suspend our interest in the philosophical past and reflect instead upon the process undertaken in developing the foregoing dialectical series, we can arrive at an important generalization. The past appeared to us under different aspects, each of which was formulated by us into what is generally referred to as "a notion, or an idea of a thing." By choice, we would have been content with one—the first. It would have been the most convenient. However, the reality confronting us— the philosophical past—would not allow this, but compelled us to mobilize, to shuttle back and forth from one aspect to the other, and likewise from one "idea" to another. Who is to blame for the inevitable labor imposed upon us—the thing itself or our own minds? Let us see.

If the reader turns his eyes to the surface of a table, or to the wall that is now perhaps in front of him, or even to this page, and if he persists awhile in this ocular inspection, he will notice something both trivial and strange. He will note that what he actually observed of the wall during the second interval does not coincide exactly with what was seen initially. This is not because the wall itself has changed during this brief period. But specks, shapes, little cracks, slight spots, shadings of color, at first unseen, are at second glance *revealed* ("revealed" being employed here in its photographic sense). In fact these appear abruptly, though one has the impression that they were there all along, though unperceived. Were the reader to feel compelled—and this is nearly impossible—

38

to conceptualize, that is to verbalize, what he saw at each interval, he would realize that the two formulas or concepts of the wall differed. This scene would be reproduced indefinitely if he continued to gaze at the wall indefinitely, the latter, like an inexhaustible spring of reality, would keep issuing forth unsuspected contents in a never-ending process of self-revelation. The object, in this instance, remained still; it is our eye that has moved, directing its visual axis first upon one section, then upon another. And with each glance cast by the eye, the wall, wounded to the core, allowed fresh aspects of itself to escape. However, even if our eye had not wandered, the same thing would have happened, because *the wall, too, makes our attention wander*. In the first moment, we would have *focused* upon certain components, in the second upon others; and each time we *focused* anew, the wall would have responded with another countenance. This is at times a compelling phenomenon of paradigmatic value. If one takes a little leaf from a tree and gazes at it persistently, at first one sees only its general outline and then the leaf itself; the leaf attracts one's gaze, propelling it, sketching one's itinerary over the surface, guiding the eyes so as to reveal the marvelous structure and the incredible geometrical, architectural grace formed by the countless tiny nerves. This, for me, was an unpremeditated, unforgettable experience—what Goethe referred to as a "Protophenomenon"—and to it I literally owe an entire dimension of my doctrine: namely, that *the thing is the master of the man*—a statement of much graver import than can be fully surmised here.[1] I must, however, add here that I have never concluded looking at a leaf.

A clearer example is perhaps offered us in looking at an

1. For an intimation of this, see my essay "Hegel's *Philosophy of History and Historiography*," 1928 [*Complete Works*, Vol. IV].

orange. At first we see only one of its *faces,* one hemi-
sphere (approximately), and then we must *move* in order
to see successive hemispheres. At each step, the appearance of the orange is different, but *connected* to its predecessor, which has already *disappeared;* with the result that
we never see the orange *all at once,* but must be content
with successive *views.* In this instance, the thing so vehe-
mently demands to be seen in its entirety that we are
impelled and literally forced to revolve around it.

There is no doubt that the orange, or reality, is directly
responsible for making us pass on from one aspect to
another, causing us displacement and effort. Obviously,
though, this occurs because at any given moment we are
able to study it only from one vantage point. If we were
ubiquitous and could see it simultaneously from all vantage points, the orange would not possess "different aspects" for us. We would see it in its totality at one glance.
Hence we are also the cause of our effort.

Our shifting motion around the orange in order to keep
seeing it would present, if the process were not silent, a
perfect analogy to the dialectical series. The quality of
our thinking, generally known as "discursive,"[2] that is,
moving by fits and starts, compels us to *traverse* reality,
step by step, making stops. At each step, we obtain one
"view" of it and these views are, on the one hand, the
intellectual *sensu stricto,* the "concepts" or "notions" or
"ideas"; and on the other, the intuitive, the correlative
"aspects" of the thing. This perusal assumes that one has
time, whereas each individual has but little, and up to now
mankind has had only one million years at its disposal.
Hence "views" of Reality have not been extremely abundant to date. One may claim that time could have been

2. The term is confusing because thinking has an intuitive aspect
and also a "logical" or conceptual aspect. This, however, is not the
proper place to delve into the question.

utilized better, for clearly a great deal of it has been wasted.[3] True, although to direct this would necessitate, among other things, determining first why history wastes so much time, why it does not progress more rapidly, why "God's mills grind away so slowly," as even Homer in his day realized.[4] In short, one must take into account not only historical time, but its divergent *tempo*, its *ritardando* and its *accelerando*, its *adagio* and its *allegro cantabile*, etc. This would result in the fantastic but obvious consequence whereby, above and beyond wasting so much time, men would be obliged to expend even more in the dedication to "*la recherche du temps perdu.*"[5]

The present occasion is not opportune for such an endeavor. Now under discussion is the fact that at any given moment we are in possession of only a limited number of cumulative views of reality. These views are simultaneous "aspects of the thing."

The "aspect" appertains to the thing; it is—to state it crudely—a piece of the thing. But it is not something relating to the thing alone; an "aspect" cannot exist without someone to behold it. Hence it is the *response* of the thing to being looked at. The act of looking collaborates in it, for that is what causes "aspects" to emerge, and since the look in each case is of a particular nature—at that moment and in that instance it looks at something *from a given point of view*— the "aspect" of the thing is insep-

3. See note 12, p. 33.
4. *Iliad*, IV, 160.
5. Furthermore, the reader who is not in the habit of *seeing* the things described by the author, but who remains on the *outside* looking at the words he utters, like at shoes in a shop window, will judge petulantly that all of this is merely a play on words. I must refer him to a forthcoming book of mine where he will find a most concrete, compact example of the literal truth of the foregoing statement, and of how one is sometimes compelled to engage in "the search for lost time" for its own sake, or for someone else's, for that of a nation or even all of mankind.

arable from the observer. Allow me to reiterate: Since in the final analysis it is always the thing, in some particular aspect, which is revealed to a point of view, these aspects pertain to the thing and are not "subjective." On the other hand, granted that they are only a *reply* to the question elicited by every look, to a given scrutiny, they are not the thing itself, but only its "aspects." According to a popular expression, we would say that the "aspect" is the "face shown" by reality. Reality puts it on for us.[6] If it were possible to integrate the countless "aspects" of a thing, we would be able to fathom the thing itself, for the thing is the "entirety." Since this is impossible, we must be content with possessing merely "aspects" of the thing and not the thing itself—as Aristotle and Saint Thomas believed.

What from the vantage point of the thing is an "aspect," from man's is the "view" taken of the thing. It is commonly called an "idea" (concept, notion, etc.). Nowadays, however, this term has only a psychological meaning, while the radical phenomenon now being discussed is in no way psychological. Undoubtedly for a thing to present its "aspects" and—what amounts to the same thing, though from the subject's standpoint—for an individual to extract his "views," all physical and psychic functions must be called into operation. Psychology, physics, and physiology examine these functions, which means however that these sciences emerge as it were from some previous thing which, in fact, is the cause of their own existence, from the primary, radical phenomenon—the presence of the thing before men's eyes in the form of "aspect" or "views." The functioning of apparatuses and mechanisms is not pertinent to our topic. It is a matter of indifference to us whether they

6. And in fact, in lieu of "aspect" one could justifiably endow the word "face" with terminological value in ontology.

function in one way or another. All that counts is the result: man is able to see things.

It is not a psychological phenomenon; far from it.[7] It is a metaphysical phenomenon, or to give it another name, an ontological one. And metaphysical phenomena—which are not mysterious or supernatural, but of the simplest, most ordinary and everyday order—are the truest phenomena or "facts" in existence, having precedence over all "scientific facts," which assume the existence of the former.

It would therefore be helpful to banish from philosophical terminology the word "idea," a word that is in its ultimate stage of deterioration and debasement, for even in psychology it does not possess a precise, authentic, unequivocal meaning. It had its great moment, its culmination, in Greece—for it is a Greek word, not a Latin one, and still less a Romanic one. It literally reigned in Syracuse with Dion, a friend and disciple of Plato, though only for a matter of days, and in Athens it was practically the "ruling" opinion for some time. It was nothing less than the *Idea*, the Platonic *Ideas*. Plato referred to their usage as "dialectics," and called it the "royal art"— ἡ βασιλικὴ Τέχνη. Who nowadays would believe it, in view of their present drab, muddled, and useless role!

7. This is not to suggest that psychology is not an intensely interesting field, one that ought to attract more individuals because of its greater accessibility, considerable rigor, and diverting quality. It can be studied with modest preparation and yield positive and creative results. Ten years ago I was eager to undertake in Spain a campaign on behalf of psychology, utilizing the enthusiasm and outstanding organizational abilities of Dr. Germain. I am not a psychologist nor could I have devoted myself to becoming one, although I have always been interested in the field and therefore could have stimulated curiosity, encouraged individuals to pursue professions in it, and fostered coteries of the studious and curious around those individuals who had already been resolutely and without support engaged in this science, particularly in Barcelona and Madrid.

Diable, qu'il a mal tourné ce mot "idée"!

The most exact rendering of the term Idea, as Plato used it, would be "aspect." And he was not concerned with psychology but with ontology. For in fact, it is in the nature of Reality to possess "aspects," "respects," and, in general, "perspective," since inherent in Reality is man standing before it and looking at it.[8] The terms perspective and knowledge are almost equivalent. However, the former is, in addition, an admonishment that knowledge is not only a *"modus cognoscentis,"* but a positive modification of that which is known—something Saint Thomas would not accept—that it is the thing transformed into mere "aspects" and only "aspects," the essence of which is to be constructed into a perspective. Knowledge—and I allude to it here only obliquely—is perspective, hence it is not a mere presentation of the thing itself in the mind, as the ancients held, nor is it the "thing itself" in the mind *per modum cognoscentis,* as the scholastics maintained, nor is it a copy of the thing, nor a construction of the thing as supposed by Kant, the positivists, and Marburg's school. But it is an "interpretation" of the thing itself, subjecting it to translation as though from one language to another—one might say from the language of being, a silent one, to the language of knowing, an articulate one. This language into which being is translated, is no more nor less than *the* language, the *logos.* Knowledge, in its ultimate and radical concretion, is dialectics—διαλέγεσθαι—*to be talking precisely about things.*

8. We shall see this at a later point. This chapter simply seeks to establish a terminology, and not to argue the truth represented therein. *Why* we speak about Reality, *why* ultimately we maintain that it has "aspects," which supposes that someone is always seeing it, etc., are fundamental themes to be treated subsequently; nevertheless, the given examples—wall, table, page of a book, leaf of a tree—are adequate *for the moment* to justify the terminology, at least in *those* instances, for the terminology effectively states what really happens.

The word enunciates the views in which the aspects of Reality appear before us.[9] What are generally referred to as "true ideas" are those that represent or correspond to realities. But this designation, aside from many other deficiencies, is contradictory, for implicit in it is an equivocal and dual use of the term "reality." On the one hand, the latter is an epistomological concept and as such, signifies simply that reality contains precisely what thought purports it to contain, or to put it differently, that the idea in fact conceptualizes that which exists in reality. If I say that the snow is white, I am saying something true because I do truly encounter in the snow that which I call "whiteness." If I say that it is black, the

9. Since knowledge is a matter between men and things, it will sometimes have to be viewed from the position of men and at other times from that of things. The subject, the viewed reality the phenomenon "knowledge"—is in both instances the same and it is only our point of view that has altered. Hence it may be helpful to have dual terms, "view" and "aspect." Finally, both terms have the advantage of being a constant reminder that thought is ultimately "seeing," *having the thing* before us—that is, *intuition.* Bear in mind that language, words, and names are concerned, aside from other functions that are not of prime importance, with two functions: first, enabling us to manipulate a large number of concepts, of ideas, in an "economical" form, thus saving us the effort of actually performing the act of thinking by means of the representative concepts and ideas. In most cases, what we carelessly classify as thinking is not precisely that, but simply its abbreviation. In this function each word is only a "token" for the actual execution of a thought, and language thereby enables us to "open an intellectual credit" with which, like great industries, we found sciences. The banking business however cannot consist solely in opening credits. This function is the correlative of another, whose claim is the meeting of due credits. Hence, the *other* function of language is the decisive one: each word is an invitation to us to *see* the thing it denominates, the thought it represents. For thought, I repeat, and will continue to repeat unceasingly in these pages, is in the ultimate and fundamental analysis "a stage of *seeing* something and *fixing* one's attention on a particular part of the thing seen." We shall therefore say that thinking means "focusing on something of that which is seen."

opposite occurs. In this sense, one is alluding to the "reality of the idea" and disregarding the "reality possessed by the thing that is real." The latter is an "ontological" concept and signifies the thing in accordance with what it is—and the thing is simply the "entirety," its integration. Hence, most of our "true ideas" represent only one of the components of the thing encountered, viewed, and apprehended by our minds at a particular moment—and therefore merely a partial, *abstract* "aspect," extirpated from the thing, though "real" in the primary sense of the term. This is the most frequent cause of our mistakes, because it leads us to believe that corroborating the truth of an idea is reduced to confirming that one "real" feature of the idea, in other words, enunciating an "authentic aspect" rather than seeking its integration by confronting the idea not only in its declared "aspect," but in its decisive nature of reality, of "being whole," and hence always possessing "additional aspects."[10]

10. Given the unavoidable parallelism between the problems of Reality and the problems of Truth, it was inevitable that the same ambiguity be reproduced in the use of the term "truth." It is too often forgotten that this word, even in most ordinary parlance, means primarily "that which is completely true" and only secondarily does it have the more modest, resigned, and partial meaning: "that which, though not completely true, is partially true because it is not an error." That "the snow is white" is in part true, because the snow does possess whiteness. First of all, however, many white things exist whose whiteness is a different shade than the snow—hence the predicate "whiteness," applied to snow, is true only if we assume it to be that particular shade, which is not made clear in the proposition and thus renders the statement an incomplete, partial truth, in jeopardy of being a false one. Secondly, it is a fact that some snows, even freshly fallen ones, are not white. Thirdly, snow is countless other things besides being white. The word "is" in the statement "the snow is . . ." likewise possesses maximum meaning that would be fulfilled only if the predicate expressed everything that the snow is. Like "reality" and "truth," however, the *is* possesses secondary and defective meanings.

3
Dialectical Series

THE ILLUSTRATION of the orange and of our own conduct in tracing the first four aspects presented by the philosophical past, constitute two "dialectical series." Our reflection on what transpired within us during those "discourses" or mental processes, provides us with a preliminary understanding of the nature of a "dialectical series." This preliminary understanding is enough to enable us to use and apply the term in this immediate context. At a later point, when we probe the subject of "thought" more deeply, we shall have to enter the crevices of reality designated by this word.

Let the term "dialectical series" not delude the reader into believing that it necessarily represents some grandiose conception, as might be indicated by its theatrical grandiloquence, reminiscent of the closest terminology of the old romantic German systems and typical of an age when philosophers were awesomely solemn and acted publicly like ventriloquists of the Absolute. We are dealing with something of no great importance and quite commonplace, though convenient.

The term is confined to designating the following sum of mental acts, which transpire in all attempts to conceptualize reality.

Every "thing" appears under one initial aspect, which leads us to a second one, then on to another, and so on in succession. For "the thing" is "in reality" the sum or *integral* of its aspects. Hence here is what we have done:

1. *Pause* before each *aspect* and obtain a view of it.

2. *Continue* thinking or move on to a contiguous aspect.

3. Not abandon—that is, *preserve*—the aspects already "viewed."

4. *Integrate* them in a sufficiently "total" view for the purposes of the subject under consideration in each particular instance.

"To pause," "to continue," "to preserve," and "to integrate" are thus the four acts exercised by dialectical thought. Each one of these acts represents a stage in our inquiry or process of understanding or thought. One could call them the *junctures* in which our knowledge of the thing is formed.

Well now, the *quid* lies in the fact that each "view" of an "aspect" demands that we advance in order to see another. The thing, as we have said, attracts us, forces us to proceed after we have paused. This new "view" prompted by the first one, is going to constitute another "aspect" of the thing—*not a random one*, however, but an aspect of the thing contiguous with the first. The "logical" contiguity of the "views" (commonly called concepts) derives from the actual contiguity of the "aspects." Thus it differs from contiguity through implication. Concept #1 is contiguous to concept #2 because it is immediately implied in the latter. Dialectical contiguity is like the concept "the space around" suggested by the concept "earth." It is contiguity through complication. Since so illustrious a thinker as Hegel referred to synthetic or complicating thought as "dialectics," I am striving by using this term to perpetuate the tradition. Observe, however, the slight relation the present instance bears to Hegel's *dialectic*.[1]

Note that in geometry the path lying between one

1. I leave for some other work an explicit explanation of what this term as it is used here and as it is used in Hegel's work have in common (very little) and in what ways they differ.

point and the adjacent point constitutes a straight line. We see then that dialectical thought *proceeds only in a straight line* and turns out to be similar to the *fen shui* or the dangerous spirits that haunted the Chinese. In fact, those entities, abettors of good and evil upon men, can be displaced only rectilinearly. Hence the edge of Chinese roofs curve upward. Otherwise, a *fen shui* installed in the roof would slide straight down and land in the garden or orchard, a highly dangerous proximity, whereas if the edge of the roof has an upward curve, the spirit's only recourse is to shoot skyward.

The contiguity of mental steps makes thinking fall into a *series* and one of the simplest sort. Clearly, then, when I refer to a "dialectical *series*" it is simply and unfortunately because what we are discussing is an ordinary, homely series, comparable to a "series of numbers," a "series of stamps," or a "series of annoyances." The fact that in this instance the series consists of thoughts, concepts, ideas, or "views" is no cause for commotion.

Let us suppose that we began pondering on any subject, great or small, and that we set down on a sheet of paper, one beneath another, the thoughts arrived at, guided through intuition or an image of the thing, until we judged it was time to stop. That will constitute the "dialectical series X" according to which X = *such and such* a subject. The subject title could be placed at the top of the page and filed accordingly in a catalogue to be available for handy reference. This is the procedure I followed in the process of writing these pages, so that none of the ideas that occurred to me would slip my mind.

Hence, the awesome term that held the promise of profound truths, reveals in the end its humble status, that of a mere cataloguing device, a memory aid for the author, a guide to assist the reader so that he would not go astray. This book is a series of dialectical series. The phenomenon could have been variously labeled. If the reader considers the lot, he will realize that the one chosen by me, despite its grandiloquent air, is the simplest and most unassuming.

This "gadget" or working tool, the dialectical series, likewise facilitates the critic's probing process, since either the numbers 1, 2, 3 . . . or the letters A, B, C . . . can be assigned to the various mental steps, thus conveniently enabling the critic to pinpoint exactly what is incomprehensible, seemingly inaccurate or needful of correction or supplementation.[2]

2. Although unable now to dwell at length upon this, I should like to note the amusing coincidence that numbering the "ideas" in a series might have with Plato's famous enigmatic "ideal numbers." There, too, a parallel series of numbers was affixed to a dialectical series of ideas, beginning with the first all-encompassing one and ending with the last concrete one—the "indivisible species" or ἄτομον εἶδος. Hence a particular number corresponds to a particular Idea—because both series are "isomorphs," as mathematicians say nowadays. In his book *Zaht und Gestalt bei Platon und Aristoteles* (1924), Stengel deciphers the twenty-three-century-old enigma of "ideal numbers" or "Ideas-numbers."

4
The Unity of Philosophy

LET US IMAGINE A pyramid and that we place ourselves
at a point situated on one of its angles. Whereupon we
take one step; that is, we move to an adjacent point either
to the right or to the left on the angle. With these two
points we have described a rectilinear direction. We continue moving from point to point, so that our movement
describes a straight line on that side of the pyramid. Suddenly, for some reason, arbitrary, convenient, or impulsive,
we halt. In principle, we could have proceeded much
farther in the same direction. This straight line is an
exact symbol for our first dialectical series, which we
shall call Series Λ.

Now, without abandoning the line we were on, let us
retrace our steps and place ourselves again at the point of
departure on the original angle. Once there, we decide
to keep going, *always in a straight line*, proceeding to the
other adjacent point which since we are going in the
opposite direction, leads us beyond the first straight line.
Since, however, we are at a tip of the angle, the other
adjacent point, even if we look for it in the same direction, is no longer on the same side of the pyramid as the
previous one. Unwittingly, therefore, in going back, we
retrace in our inverse itinerary the *original* point of departure and pass on, not only to another point, but to
another side of the pyramid.

This is what we shall now do. Maintaining strict continuity of thought, we shall take another look at the
original phenomena—the philosophical past—this time in

another direction, observing another of its facets, so that the series of aspects which thereupon emerge before us will be exceedingly different from the first. Thus, departing once again from the panorama of the history of philosophy, we shall produce a new straight mental line, a second "dialectical series," which we shall call Series B.

If you recall, according to the "first aspect" the philosophical past resembled a "multitude of opinions about itself." It was the first view we had of that reality, and first views are normally taken from a distance.[1] Everything seems confused. We shall see how "confusion" is an initial phase of all knowledge, *without which one cannot progress to clarity*. The important thing for the individual who truly desires to think is that he not be overly hurried but be faithful at each step of his mental itinerary to the aspect of reality currently under view, that he *strive to avoid disdain for the preliminary distant and confused aspects* due to some snob sense of urgency impelling him to arrive immediately at the more refined conclusions.

In fact, the thing that was initially attractive about this "multitude of opinions on the same thing" was the notion "multitude." We viewed the philosophical past as a drip of water in which an infusion of doctrines swarmed chaotically, without order or harmony, in open divergence and universal babble, in mutual conflict. The scene was one of infinite mental upheaval. The history of philosophy, in fact, has—and there is no reason for hiding it—the amusing aspect of a pleasant insane asylum. Philosophy, though it holds the promise of providing maximum

1. When this is not the case it means that the encounter is abnormal and that reality presented to us is immediate, clear, and precise. This produces such a *choc* in individuals that it elicits an anomalous phenomenon—both in the good and the pejorative sense. One of these is the strange, sudden crisis known as "conversion," another "sudden ecstasy," another "bewilderment," etc.

logic—"truth," "reason"—momentarily and in its historical entirety, shows characteristics similar to insanity.
The reader ought to become accustomed to such meta-
morphoses, for he will witness many in this book.[2]

Obsessed by this multitudinous, divergent character,
we noticed nothing else and were inevitably carried in
the direction of Series A. But now having grown accustomed to the apparent plurality and discrepancy of philosophies, and having intellectually mastered them and
become convinced that in the end "there is no such thing,"
we can disconcern ourselves with that notion at least for
awhile, and confront another. Namely, that despite the
existence of many divergent opinions, all are opinions *on
the same thing*. This invites us to try to detect amid the
multitude of philosophies some unity, and even a *oneness*
in *philosophy;* to discover what the diverse doctrines have
in common. Otherwise it would be meaningless to call those
doctrines, despite their divergences, "philosophies" or any
similar name. Employing the term implies that beneath
their antagonistic masks, all are *essentially* philosophy—
that is, that philosophies are not a mere jumble of this,
that, and the other, but that all possess ultimately a unity.
That is, we hope, suspect, and presume that they do.

Let us then jovially set forth on the rugged journey in
search of philosophy's unity. We will notice at once that
this new jaunt leads us inward into philosophies, toward
their core, an "inside," an inwardness and reconditeness,
in comparison with Series A where everything viewed
was extrinsic, external, dermato-skeletal.

Well then, how shall we proceed? The reader perhaps

2. The reason for this is exceedingly simple. Since it is characteristic of reality to reveal different aspects depending upon
where and how one regards it, each of these constitutes a "form"
or figure, a "morphon" that reality assumes, and when perceived
by us, is interpreted as its "transformation," "transfiguration," or
"metamorphosis."

may think that we ought to *commence* by taking each philosophy one by one, in chronological order, and examine "its interior." Thus we might compare the core of each and determine whether or not they coincide, whether the *same* interior serves many different bodies.

In the first place this would not constitute a panoramic, total gaze at the *entire* philosophical past, which is the course we decided to pursue at the conclusion of Marías' book and which, as we said, was a sort of farewell to that continent of the past. In the second place, probing deeply into each doctrine would mean we were being untrue to our first view, which was concerned with the *unity* of philosophy, and though it presents an exceedingly modest aspect, it should not be omitted. The foundation and progress of science can be attributed to not skipping over modest aspects. Physics exists because mathematical astronomy exists and this, in turn, because Kepler spent years respectfully and devoutly immersed in the absurd five-minute arc of discrepancy that existed in the observation data regarding the position of the planets, which had been noted with prodigious detail by Tycho-Brahe in his "first solution" to the system of their movements around the sun. According to the latter fallacious solution the planets still described circular orbits. During an impassioned labor of years Kepler's circumferences, divergent from Tycho's data, became flattened, mollified, slightly elongated, and finally resulted in the famous ellipses that existed among mankind until Einstein's time. Those ellipses, in combination with Galileo's mechanical laws, certain general Cartesian methods, and additional subsequent factors, made possible the concept of gravity and with it "Newtonian philosophy," the first authentic system, one whose attainment derived from thought and dealt with something real that man possessed. In other words, it was the first effective science.

And that is to say nothing if we turn our attention to the minute differences—in comparison to which Kepler's "five minutes" seem gigantic—whose religious contemplation resulted in the theory of relativity. And furthermore, if we regard the matter from another side, an even more modest one, and note that the work of Kepler, a genial man, would have been impossible if Tycho-Brahe, a man who was not a genius—unless genius be thought of simply as patience—had not earlier devoted his whole life to the humble task of gathering the most exact measurements possible at that time on sidereal displacements, and this in turn would have been impossible had an even humbler man not been born in Portugal, a nation of fantastic imprecision. This good man, Núñez, who doggedly persisted in inventing an instrument to measure millimeter decimals, the ingenious and renowned *nonius* that preserves forever, in Latin mummification, the humble name of our neighbor Núñez.[3] Let us therefore give due consideration, at least in the essentials, to the first *aspect* of the philosophical past presented to us by this new *respect* or facet—the "unity" of philosophies.[4]

3. Vice versa—as we shall subsequently see—had Kepler encountered metrical data of greater exactitude, even though it in no way approached the fabulous precision attained by contemporary physics, he would have failed, and physics would not have been founded, for the mathematical resources at that time were not sufficient to master such small complex differences. This indicates the extent to which science is a highly delicate organism whose members, though disparate in nature, must advance with a sort of "preordained harmony."

4. Nothing would be easier than to achieve this intent. It would be merely a matter of pages. The limits of this book however, and the abundance of material, oblige me in what herein follows, to intersperse things that *rigorously speaking* pertain to more recent, proximate aspects, which are not seen from a bird's eye view, though that strictly is what belongs in this chapter. It is necessary, however, for purely didactic reasons, to anticipate certain things. What really matters is that everything essential to this aspect be

With respect to things definitely past, our first *view* is generally not of a visual nature; it is neither ocular nor is it of the mental order we shall subsequently examine under the term "intuition." We can only have a view of something that "is there in person before us" in one guise or other, either close or at a distance. A view constitutes the immediate relation between our minds and a thing, and from the moment we descry it upon the distant horizon until it is directly within eye's reach, we merely glide over forms that become increasingly precise and clear in their direct relation to that thing. The radical past, however, consists in that which "is not directly before us." It consists in that which is gone, in that which *par excellence* is absent. Our first and most elementary notice of it is not in *seeing* it but in *hearing* about it. Thus in philosophy, the first thing if any, which we the living encounter is the series of terms, book titles, and individual names that was *involved* in philosophizing. The past is transmitted to us via names and things that we have heard about it—through tradition, fables, legend, chronicles, or history—sayings, sheer sayings. Hence the first contact with philosophy stems from what "is said" about it. The Greeks called what was "said" about something "fame"—in the sense of our own popular expression "fame has it . . . "

In addition there exists a relative past, one that is in some degree still present—one might say it is a past that

---

said and as long as that is accomplished, no harm is done if certain inessential things are included. Besides—and this admonition holds true for the entire chapter—insofar as the strict phenomenon of "philosophy seen from a distance" is concerned, the addition of these closer views emanating from someone immersed in philosophy, someone with more than a vague and remote inkling of it, can only serve to suggest the explicit nature of philosophy to the "uninformed," those who are unable to articulate it but who see, hear, and vaguely sense it.

has not vanished totally. We retain a certain visual relationship with this past, and can still dimly perceive it.
The wrinkles on an old man's face inform us that he is a
living, present past. We don't have to be *told* that the man
existed: the fact that he existed before we did is forcefully
evident. This likewise occurs with ruin-covered landscapes, with faded, tattered clothes, with ancient volcanic
mountains the only remain of which is a stony skeleton,
with our Tagus River, imprisoned in its narrow bed and
gashed into the hardness of the rocks. With our own eyes
we can see, if we have the slightest talent for physiog-
nomy, that the Tagus is an ancient river, a senescent
stream, flowing weakly along its hardened, calloused
river bed—in short, we are witnesses to the spectacle of
fluvial arteriosclerosis. (Anyone who is not grieved, or
at least saddened, by the sight of this decrepit river that
runs past Toledo, is either inherently blind, unworthy of
existence, or if he must exist, unworthy of peering at the
world. It is futile; he sees nothing.)

I repeat, however, that the closest most normal channel
of information[5] about the historical past is through names.
The phenomenon is not peculiar to this particular situation. Names constitute the form of the distant, the
radically distant, relationship between our minds and
things. The first communication we receive of most things
and our only one of a great number of them is their
names, and only their names.

They emerge abruptly, drift into our ears when the
things therein designated are utterly removed from us—

5. In instances where the sole remains of the past are material
objects—artifacts, stones—and not verbal remains, we always sense
a lack of its inwardness. Hence—thanks primarily to recent
advances in research—we are confronted with entire mute civiliza-
tions, whose vestiges are present like a hieroglyph for which
meaning must be found. This is the difference between prehistory
and archeology on the one hand and philology on the other.

invisible, perhaps forever, on some faraway horizon. Names thus are like the birds one sees on the high seas, which fly out of nowhere toward the navigator, forewarning him of the presence of islands. Words, in fact, are announcements, a promise of the thing, and in fact a *modicum* of the thing. The Eskimo theory whereby Man is a composite of three elements: body, soul, and . . . name is not as extravagant as appears. The ancient Egyptians held the same belief. Further, one must not forget "Where two or three are gathered together *in my name, there am I* in the midst of them" (Matthew 18:20).[6]

Names are a "reference to things." They stand in their stead, in place of them. Language therefore is a symbol. Something is symbolic when its presence serves *as* a representative for another thing that is not present, something that we do not have before us. *Aliquid stat pro aliquo*—is the symbolic relationship. The word is thus the presence of the thing that is absent. This is its genius —it permits a reality to continue to exist in some way in the place from which it has gone or where it never even was. The "Himalayas," for example, conveys to me here, in Estoril, where the only mountain in view is the puny Cintra—it conveys to me "something akin" to the Himalayas, a vague shadowy spectral form of its huge bulk. And while as we now *talk about* the Himalayas, we possess it, in some small measure, we tread it, we are in contact with it—that is, we are in contact *about* it.

However, the presence endowed by the word to the absent object is, of course, neither solid nor real. The representative never is the thing represented. Hence as soon as a chief of state arrives in a foreign country, his

6. See elsewhere on *Magical Logic and Ontology*, where I discuss the phenomena whereby men regard thought = logos = word as having derived from the individual and as residing in him. [The epigraph alluded to was apparently never written.—*Ed.*]

ambassador in that country ceases to exist. That's how
things are! A name, with respect to the thing named, represents, at best, only an outline, an abbreviation, a
skeleton, an extract: its concept. That, *if* properly understood, is not such a soft task!

Hence a word's magical power of enabling a thing to
be simultaneously in two extremely remote places—there
where it actually is, and there where it is being discussed
—should be held in rather low esteem. For what we have
of the thing, when we have its name, is a caricature: its
concept. And unless we proceed with caution, unless we
evince distrust for words and attempt to pursue the things
themselves, the names will be transformed into masks,
which instead of enabling the thing to be in some way
present for us, will conceal the thing from us. While the
former is the magical gift of words, their feat, the latter
is their disgrace, the thing language constantly verges on
—a masquerade, a farce, mere jabber.

Whether we like it or not, though, the only thing that
each of us possesses of most things is its niggardly nomi-
nal mask—"words, words, words"—emanations, drafts,
gusts wafted by the social atmosphere, which we infuse
and which are lodged within us through inhalation.
Whereupon—because we possess the names of things—
we think that we can *talk* from them and about them.
And then someone comes along and says to us, "Let's
talk *seriously* about such and such a thing." As if that
were possible! As if "talking" were something that could
be done with ultimate radical seriousness and not with the
pained conscience of someone performing a farce! If one
truly wishes to do something *seriously* the first injunction
is to keep quiet. True knowledge, as we shall methodically
see, is silence and reserve.

5

The Authentic Name*

LET US TURN NOW to the various names that have been given to this occupation which Western man has pursued for twenty-six centuries, to the books that have perpetuated it, and to the appellations and nicknames linguistically imposed upon its practitioners.

Philosophy as such begins with Parmenides and Heraclitus. Its predecessors—Ionian "physiology," Pythagorism, Orpheism, Hecataeus—constitute a prelude and nothing more, *Vorspiel und Tanz.*

Parmenides and others of his day named the subject that they expounded "aletheia." This was philosophy's original name. Now the moment a name is born, the moment something for the first time is *called* by a word, is a moment of exceptional creative purity. The thing stands before Man still devoid of designation, without a vestige of nomenclature, ontologically out in the raw, one might say. No ideas, interpretations, words, or clichés exist yet between it and Man. A means must be found to express it, to articulate it, to transpose the element and "world" of concepts, *logoi,* or words. Which to choose? Let us note in passing something we shall examine thoroughly at a later point. *The question of creating a word.* Language is precisely something not created by the individual but something that is found by him, previously established by his social environs, his tribe, *polis,* city, or nation. The words of a language have their meaning imposed by col-

* [Title supplied.—*Ed.*]

lective usage. Speaking is a re-using of that accepted meaning, *saying what is already known*, what everyone knows, what is mutually known. We are now dealing, however, with a new entity, one that has no usual name. Finding a denomination for it cannot be regarded as "talking," because no word yet exists for it—it is "talking to oneself." Only one person is beholding the "new thing," and in selecting a word to name it, only he understands it. Hence we are witnessing a function of speech that is the opposite of language—that is, what people say or what is commonly known.[1] Now it is necessary for the person himself who sees the thing *for the first time* to understand some commonplace everyday expression, a word whose meaning is *analagous*—which is all it can be —to the "new thing." The analogy, though, is a transposition of meaning; it is a metaphorical use of the word, hence, a poetic one. When Aristotle discovered that everything is "made of something,"[2] the way chairs, tables, and doors are made of wood, he called the substance *from which* (Τὸ ἐξ οὗ) all things are made, "wood"—ὕλη— understood as wood par excellence, the ultimate and universal "wood" or "matter." Our word *matter* is simply wood (in Spanish, *madera*) metaphorized.

Hence it turns out—and who would have thought so! —that coming upon a technical term for a new rigorous concept, the creation of a terminology is simply a poetic process.

Vice versa, if we revivify the definition of a technical term, once it is determined, and attempt to understand its essence, we resuscitate the then existent vital situation of

1. A systematic treatment of language is to be found in a yet unpublished work of mine, *Man and People*, wherein its social aspect is examined in the light of my sociological doctrine [*Man and People*, Chapters XI and XII].
2. Strictly speaking, the term was created before Aristotle.

the bygone thinker who *saw* the "new thing" before him for the first time.

This circumstance, this vital experience in new Greek thought, later to be known as philosophizing, was aptly named by Parmenides and alert groups of his day as "aletheia."[3] In speculating on some ordinary, prosaic, accepted ideas on reality, he discovered them to be false but that one could discern behind them the reality itself, appearing *as if* a concealing crust or veil or covering had been removed, thus allowing the reality to emerge un-clothed, naked, and patent. Thus, in the thinking process, his mind had performed something *akin to* un-dressing, un-covering, removing a veil or covering, re-vealing (= un-veiling), de-ciphering an enigma or hieroglyphic.[4] This literally is what the word *a-letheia* meant in *popular language*—discovery, exposure, denudation, revelation. By A.D. 1, with the advent of another radical discovery, a new, great, and different philosophical revelation, the word *aletheia* had in seven centuries of philosophy expended its fresh metaphorical import, and another term had to be found for "revelation." This, in tune with the Asiatic tenor of the times, was a Baroque word—*apokalipsis*—which has exactly the same, though reinforced, meaning as *aletheia*.

Aletheia, meanwhile, presents philosophy for what it is—an endeavor at discovery and at deciphering enigmas to place us in contact with the naked reality itself. *Aletheia* signifies *truth*. For *truth* must not be regarded as the dead thing that twenty-six centuries of custom and inertia would have us believe, but as a verb—something alive,

---

3. In the two or three previous generations—Ionian—the word ἱστορεῖν (to recount) expresses what they did, which subsequently from a retrospective technical viewpoint was called φυσιολογία (natural science).

4. See *Meditations on Quixote*, 1914 [*Complete Works*, Vol. I; in English translation, New York, W. W. Norton & Co., Inc., 1961].

something at its moment of attainment, of birth; in short, as action. Current vigorous terms for expressing *aletheia* = truth are: inquiry, quest for truth—that is, for the naked reality that is concealed behind the robes of false-hood. Due to some curious contamination between that which is un-covered = reality, and our act of un-covering or denuding it, we often speak about the "naked truth," a tautology. That which is naked is reality and denuding it is the truth, inquiry, or *aletheia*.

This, the original name of philosophy, is its true or authentic name[5] and thus its poetic name. The poetic name is the one we employ when inwardly referring to something, when talking to ourselves in secret *endophasia*, or inner speech. Ordinarily, however, we do not have the ability to create those secret inner names whereby we would understand ourselves with respect to things, and we would say what they authentically *are to us*. We suffer in our soliloquies from muteness.

The poet's role hinges upon his ability to create that inner tongue, that wondrous *argot* comprised of only authentic names. It turns out, as we read him, that the poet's inner self as transmitted via his poetry—be it verse or prose—coincides to a great extent with our own. That is why we understand him: he provides the language for our inner selves and thereby enables us to understand ourselves. Hence the strange phenomenon whereby the pleasure aroused by poetry and admiration for the poet stem, paradoxically, from our notion of being plagiarized. Everything he tells us we have previously "felt," except that we did not know how to express it.[6] The poet is the

5. It seems incredible that current linguistics still ignores the fact that things do have "authentic names" and believes this to be incompatible with the essentially changeable nature of language, which is comprised almost of sheer accident.

6. What would happen to this normal, fundamental phenomenon of human life at a time when ordinary men, mass-men, became progressively petulant? As a matter of fact, something very amus-

shrewd go-between with Man and himself.

"Truth," or "inquiry," ought to have been philosophy's everlasting name. Nevertheless, it was called thus only in its initial phase, that is, when the "thing itself"—in this case, philosophizing—was a new pursuit, one still unfamiliar to people, devoid of a public existence, unable to be seen from the outside. It was the authentic sincere name privately given by the philosopher to what he found himself doing, something that had not existed for him earlier. He was alone with reality—"*his* philosophizing"—confronting it, in a state of grace before it, and *without any social precaution*, he innocently gave it its true name, the way those "terrible" poets, children, would do.

But no sooner did philosophizing become a repetitive occurrence, an habitual occupation, and people began seeing it from the outside—the way people always see everything—than the situation changed. No longer was the philosopher alone with the phenomena in the intimacy of his philosophizing, but in addition to being a philosopher, he became a public figure, like a magistrate, a priest, a doctor, a merchant, a soldier, a jester, an executioner. That irresponsible impersonal character, social milieu, that monster of n + 1 heads, people, began to respond to the new reality: the "inquirer," that is, the philosopher. And since the essence of the latter—philosophizing—was a much more inward labor than all other callings, the clash between one's outer social guise and

---

ing, which I have seen happen with increasing intensity and frequency, often to an astonishing extent among the younger generations: when a young person today reads and understands us, he immediately *thinks that the idea occurred to him*. Just as the writer, if he truly is one, appears to "plagiarize" the reader, so today's impertinent reader seriously believes that he is the true author and knew it all before. This is a stupefying and grotesque but nonetheless undeniable phenomenon.

one's inner self was greater. Then "things began to happen" to the word "aletheia," or "inquiry," a newborn word, one still so utterly childlike, tremulous, and devoid of subtlety. Words, which after all are modes of human existence, also have their "mode of life." And since inherent in life is "having things happen," a word is no sooner born, than it is plunged into a rugged series of adventures, some favorable and others adverse,[7] until its final disappearance and demise.

When the noun "aletheia" was invented for private use, attacks from the outside world were unforeseen and hence it was defenseless in this respect. For no sooner were people aware of the existence of philosophers, or "inquirers," than they began assaulting them, misinterpreting them, confusing them with other vague professions, whereupon that marvelous, ingenuous name had to be abandoned and another assumed, one born of spontaneous generation, infinitely inferior but more "practical"—that is, a more inane, base, and cautious one. Now it no longer was a question of naming the naked reality "to philosophize"— that is, the thinker and it in solitude. The neighbors and other people intervened—awful characters—and the name had to have an eye on two fronts, it had to look to two sides—at reality and at other men—to name the thing not for one person alone but the *Others* as well. Looking in two directions, however, means being cross-eyed. Let us now observe how this cross-eyed, absurd name, Philosophy, was born.

7. Recall the former brief allusion to the adventures that befell the word "idea." Each word, in principle, possesses a biography, the term used somewhat analogously as it is used with reference to men. The reason that it is only *analogous* is that words, finally, pertain to "collective existence," which is analogous to "personal existence," the only true life. [See *Man and People*.]

6
Philosophy Embarks on the Discovery of Another World[1]

IN ITS FIRST ASPECT—the verbal aspect—the philosophical past, comprised of commonly heard names, gave the impression of being a rather confused field. It gave no inkling of the unity sought for in philosophy. On the contrary, things that were quite similar appeared under extremely dissimilar names, and things that were most dissimilar under the same name. In sum, a hazy blurred image emerged in which one perceived the throb of divergent impulses. We would be wrong however in deducing that the discovery of multiplicity rather than the sought for unity meant that our time had been wasted. In general, we must rely on the following rule, which for the time being seeks merely to be a practical prescription and perhaps simultaneously a tautology: "It is impossible for any aspect of reality, if scrupulously analyzed, not to convey some truth—a truth that is not only true but one that must be taken into account, and which will acquire its full meaning at perhaps a much later juncture in our progressive thinking."

Advancing from the "absent presence" or the names

1. [According to the manuscript, this chapter concludes *The Origin of Philosophy*. Chapters VII and X were written at a later date, and together with the intermediary ones—Chapters VIII and IX—form the *Fragments on the Origin of Philosophy* alluded to in the Preliminary Note.—*Ed.*]

for philosophical reality, which though now present, are in the remote distance and on the most distant horizon where objects become clouds, we have been viewing philosophical doctrines externally, like plastic images, figures, or myths. Since Philosophy is thought, and hence interiority, no view of it can be more inadequate than one that views it simply as exteriority and sheer spectacle. The second aspect of it more than illuminates the first, for behind the strange divergent landscapes and fauna just presented by the mass of philosophies, we are now able to discern the persistent existence of two worlds, the manifest world and the latent or supra-world. The latent world pulsates beneath the manifest world and its revelation constitutes the supreme philosophical task. Thus philosophy begins by bisecting a seemingly single world; that is, in an apparently inverted operation, it duplicates the world that there was and elicits another behind or over it. The result, whether it be through bisection or duplication, is the same: philosophy leaves us with two worlds on our hands. The relationship between the two worlds can be highly disparate. They may show no contact whatsoever and as we shall presently see, appear to be back to back. On the other hand, they may be intermingled or involucrated so that the latent world is revealed by viewing the manifest world. In short, both may remain distant but connected, in continual cross-reference to each other, a reference that merely serves to corroborate their separation.

So commanding is the persistent duality of worlds that, despite the inadequate view of philosophy to be derived from the second aspect and the irresponsibility of our impression, it cannot help but stimulate our attention. This attention aroused in us by what is seen, whether we want it to or not, simultaneously whets our curiosity. Our minds mobilize and move one step forward in order to view the thing more clearly.

The orange incited us to move around it in order to juxtapose the aspects of its spheroidal body. Its successive aspects, though different, were all on the same plane, or equidistant from us. The radius of our *views* around the orange was equal.[2]

In the present dialectical series, however, we announced from the outset that our mental vector would proceed in a penetrating sense. We were going to advance from the extreme "outside"—names—to the extreme "inside"— the unity of philosophy. This third stage, inspired by curiosity to learn why philosophy is not content with one world, the habitual one, but divides or superimpregnates it, compels us to shuttle across the dividing line which, like a frontier, separates philosophy's "outside" from its "inside," its outer image from its innermost essential condition, its interiority. To do this we must for the first time abandon our panoramic contemplation of the philosophical past and, in principle, halt before each philosophy, penetrate it—in short, study it.

(This, however, would be tantamount to retracing the history of philosophy, a senseless repetition of Julián Marías' book.)

What would make sense for our present aim would be a thorough analysis of the exemplary beginning of the philosophical profession, to attain maximum understanding of early philosophy; to learn thereby precisely why it dualizes the world and how it calls forth, discovers, or invents the latent world, the strange, nonhabitual world that is characteristic of philosophy; then once this information is isolated, to pursue, at its decisive moments, the *variation produced by this dual operation throughout the*

---

2. Otherwise we would combine aspects of the spheroid from different distances and our resulting image of the orange would be deformed because of the lack of unity in perspective.

history of philosophy up to the present. This would fur-
nish us with philosophy's unity in the past. Confronted by
its past unity, clearly defined and unequivocal, and led
thus into the "immediate past" or the present, we can
then determine what ought to be done in the future. Our
backward gaze will have fulfilled its mission and we will
be ready to turn our attention forward.

Historians are horrified by chance. It piques and offends
them because in their opinion—the childish opinion typical of historians—chance represents the negation of historical science insofar as it is the enemy of "reason."
Moreover, since chance is constantly on the prowl between the lines of their writing like an *enfant terrible,*
chucking them under the chin and laughing at their "reason," they regard it not only as the enemy of any potential
history but as a terribly insolent entity whose perpetual
presence and cynical self-exhibition lacks the decorum of
science. Clearly, however, future historians who—finally!
—will be true historians, will not hesitate when encoun-
tering chance as a component of reality, to recognize it
and to emphasize its presence and influence, to the same
extent as other historical "forces." That is, they will dis-
regard what traditional usage, tyrannized by logicians and
mathematicians, referred to as "reason," and they will
resolve to understand the historical reality and the reason
that is inherent in it and that is addressed to us, which
henceforth we shall call "historical reason." This book
will gradually confront us with that reason of the future,
which is markedly different from venerable "pure reason,"
but nonetheless is the exact opposite of vagueries, meta-
phors, utopias, and mysticisms. It is therefore a reason
that is much more rational than the old one, in which
"pure reason" appeared as an insensate enchantress, and
in accordance with this reason many things that hereto-

fore were considered irrational will cease to suffer from this pejorative label. In short, suffice it to say now that historical reason, prepared to swallow reality without repulsion, squeamishness, or scruples, manages to provide a contour of rationality even to chance, heretofore the demon of irrationality and the *ci-devant* enemy of history.

Philosophy itself begins with a monumental coincidence, for it begins simultaneously, possibly even *exactly* on the date, with the appearance of two men who, though they belong to the same generation,[3] inhabit diametric poles of the Greek world—Eleusis and Ephesus—and it begins in each in two opposite directions so that the doctrines of these two men at once and forever represent the two most antagonistically conceivable forms of philosophy, as though *someone*—Chance?—had taken pleasure in leaving all of future philosophy from its very outset in this initial divided position.[4]

Thus it is simply a question of didactic convenience whether one begins an exposition of early philosophy with the one or the other figure, and in the present instance there can be no room for doubt. Parmenides, that madman of Reason, offers a perfect entry into the vast extravagance of philosophy, transmitting with peerless radicalism the liveliest impression of and lack of sense in Logic.

Our exposition of Parmenides' doctrine may possibly turn out to be more complete than heretofore existing ones, for one must not lose sight of the concrete urgency

3. By "generation" I mean a *given* fifteen-year period. [See *Man and Crisis, Complete Works,* Vol. V.]

4. It is not within the scope of this book to delve into the chronological question posed by the life of both philosophers. Suffice it to indicate that the greater comprehension one has of each, the less evident is the (mutual) reference to and presumed polemics of Parmenides and Heraclitus. On the other hand, examination and comparison of biographical data increasingly confirm the trend initiated twenty years ago by Reinhardt to consider them as strict contemporaries.

of our interest in it. We are not engaged in detailing the history of philosophy, but in reflecting upon it to discover amid its vast exuberance the unity of this discipline. The first symptom encountered in our panoramic survey was the duality of worlds displayed by philosophy, leading us thereupon to an inner study of early philosophy with the precise intention of learning why the latter is not content with the habitual world but divides or duplicates it. This then is one focal question in the interpretation of fragments from Parmenides. Anything else we learn will be additional and gratuitous, but not the result of deliberate inquiry.

Approaching the Parmenides fragments with this predetermined wariness, we are beset by a prior doubt. Is philosophy, in fact, the first to divide and duplicate the world, or was a bisection previously performed by antecedent disciplines? This question, an indispensable one, must be peremptorily answered in the following manner: We do not know whether a dual world existed prior to philosophy, but we are presently unable to resolve our ignorance inasmuch as we would then be obliged to examine chronological periods prior to the history of philosophy, failing thereby to adhere to the aspect before us, whose only past horizon is the philosophical past. Once before[5] we had occasion to suspect that eventually we would be compelled to extend our temporal panorama of Man's intellectual comportment into the more remote and dense past to make a thorough scrutiny of how Man employed his mind before he began philosophizing. Methodologically, however, this would be inexcusable before having exhausted what the strict philosophical past can yield. We have still not extracted anything of true value from the latter. Its exploitation has only begun. Hence, adhering to the rule of faithfulness to the aspect in view,

5. See *Notes on Thinking* [*Complete Works*, Vol. V].

let us confine ourselves to the texts of early philosophy in order to try to extract from them an initial explanation regarding the "unity" of philosophy. The issue of what transpired prior to the advent of philosophy and whether the world had by then been divided, does not therefore concern us, for although it possibly was, the reasons for its division were not the same immediate reasons for which philosophy divides and duplicates it, and by virtue of which it is born.

Parmenides' text itself will reveal what those two worlds are and why philosophy separates them. But *adhering strictly* to a text, to what a thinker says, can mean two highly different things: adhering to what is actually said; adhering to the thinker's thought as a whole, but *without* going beyond it to find precursors in other thinkers and in collective thought.

We shall take the latter course, what I consider *adhering strictly* to a text. For the first—confining ourselves literally to the textual content—would limit our understanding of that particular text and the assimilation of the thought therein expressed. Furthermore it would ignore the universal law of language whereby no statement is an adequate summation of its intention, but merely an abbreviation, an insinuation of what it *means to say*.[6] All articulated language partially states or considers as stated many things that act upon the thinker, that *form part* of his thought but are either "left unsaid because they are assumed" or that he himself, because they seem so self-evident to him, neglects to pursue.

Some of these tacit suppositions that Parmenides never pursued—which he did not dismember and examine individually—must be made evident, brought out into the open, or this Greek thinker may not be understood. One

6. See the chapter "La reviviscencia de los cuadros." [*Papeles sobre Velázquez y Goya*, Madrid, Revista de Occidente, 1950.]

must realize that these suppositions do not actually constitute thinking *prior* to Parmenides, for prior implies only that which was and has ceased to be. Those suppositions that operated prior to Parmenides, continued to operate in him as they did after him and in fact until the period of philosophical thought came to an end in Greece. They do not therefore constitute a "before" or an "after" but an "always" in relation to Greek intellectual comportment. Hence they are to be found in all Hellenic doctrine as an ever-present actuality.

There are other things, however, that are not permanent even in this relative sense, which are recent acquisitions of collective thought, and which nevertheless constitute for a particular thinker tacit suppositions or are merely incidentally expressed in his work. They are his "immediate historical implications." These implications have to be made manifest and precise in order to understand a text, because they are its basic context.[7]

Stated with ultimate sobriety, this means: a thinker's ideas always possess a *subsoil*, a *soil*, and an *adversary*. None of these three entities is, literally, what is expressed in a thinker's work. They remain peripheral, and the thinker barely ever alludes to them. But in order to understand him, they must be filled in. Every text is a fragment of an unexpressed context.

The *subsoil*, composed of deep layers rooted in ancient collective thought from which a particular thinker derives his ideas, is generally something he is unconscious of. The *soil* is of recent creation—the fundamental, newly founded ideas accepted by the thinker. It is the soil in which he is grounded, and from which his own unique thought and ideas stem. Hence he does not refer to it, just as one does not indicate to people the ground upon

7. An exposition of what I call "categories of context" may be found in Chapters X and XII of *Man and People*.

which one's feet tread at each moment. Finally, all thought represents *thought against*, whether so indicated verbally or not. Our creative thought is always shaped in opposition to some other thought, which we believe erroneous, fallacious, and needful of correction. I call this the *adversary*, a menacing bluff, which at a particular moment looms above our soil, and hence, *likewise emerges from that soil*, and in contrast with which the configuration of our own doctrine takes form. The adversary is never an ineffectual past: it is always contemporary and seemingly vestigial.

This sober distinction allows us to detail with complete rigor that which mandatorily must be appended to Parmenides' text—the definition of his soil and of his adversary—and of something else that temporarily will not be explored, though *ultimately*, at the proper moment, it too will have to be reconstructed, to wit, his subsoil. This, however, is not the time for it. For the present, we shall confine ourselves to the minimum context, our commentary limited only to what the thinker had in view, that which he directly and clearly depended upon; hence, what he considered as his soil and his enemy.

7
Man's Permanent Possibilities*

IN THE PAGES entitled "The Essence of Philosophy," Dilthey endeavors to concretize the concept of philosophy, and to do this he compares, connects, and contraposes the field of philosophy with religion and poetry, applying the latter in the larger sense of literature. In reading these admirable pages, one thing is especially striking: religion, philosophy, and literature, vital functions of the human mind, appear as permanent possibilities in man. That precisely is what one finds surprising about Dilthey, who more radically than his predecessors—Hegel and Comte—taught us to view historicity as a constitutive element in the human being. The apparent implication of historicity is that all truly human entities are born one fine day and die another. Nothing truly human if it is at all real, and hence, concrete, can be permanent. This does not mean that there is nothing constant in man. Otherwise we could not talk about mankind, human life, the human being. In other words, man has an invariable structure which traverses all of his changes. That structure is not real, however, since it is not concrete, but abstract. It consists in a system of abstract moments, which as such, demand to be integrated in each instance with variable determi-

* [As was noted in footnote 1 of Chapter VI, Chapter VII was written after Chapters VIII and IX and inserted when Ortega was writing the text that he prepared for homage to Jaspers. The aforementioned *Fragments on the Origin of Philosophy,* published in German, contains Chapters VII to X of this book. Thus not only is it incomplete, but its pages moreover were presented by the author as "fragments."—*Ed.*]

nants in order for the abstraction to be transformed into reality. If we say that man always lives from certain beliefs, we are enunciating a truth that is a theorem pertaining to the Theory of Life, but that truth does not affirm anything real; rather it manifests its own unreality by leaving indeterminate the belief that he lives in every instance, and is like an algebraic formula, a constant appeal for us to fill in the *empty places—leere Stelle.*

In the light of this prefatory warning, the terms "religion," "philosophy," and "poetry" acquire an equivocal meaning because one is uncertain whether they designate abstractions or real forms adapted by life. And, in fact, Dilthey's pages are filled with an incessant semantic reverberation because the terms jump continually from their abstract meaning to their concrete meaning and vice versa. This terminological indecisiveness was exacerbated by a general proclivity toward an impoverished vocabulary displayed by the so-called "sciences of the mind." I have elsewhere commented on the potential harm of employing the same word—"poetry"—to designate the work of both Homer and Verlaine. This likewise occurs with words like "philosophy" and "religion." Obviously, the conceptual meaning of these nouns ought to be sufficiently vague and formal so that they may embrace the most diverse and even contrary aspects. In principle there would be no reason to criticize this course were it not for the fact that we thereupon find the same word employed as a proper noun to designate very concrete forms of human occupation. The problem has a certain contemporary significance for philosophy because Western thought—and I refer to the best of it—has of late, under this name, comported itself in forms where the designation "philosophy" becomes highly questionable. Without attempting at the moment to formalize an opinion on this matter, I merely wish to suggest the possibility that what we are now beginning to engage in under the traditional aegis of philosophy is not another philosophy but something new and different from all philosophy.

The fact is that when Dilthey finally pinpoints what he means by philosophy, he is describing a manner in which mental mechanisms function, something that has not always operated in the history of mankind but that came about one fine day in Greece and has indeed come down to us—with no guarantee, however, of its perpetuation.

Notwithstanding, we make no claim to having solved the problem of whether those pursuits are or are not permanent possibilities in man. We have done exactly the opposite—opened the subject in a somewhat peremptory form.

Before embarking on any systematic considerations, we ought to examine the religious attitude that confronted the innovators of philosophy. This moment in Greek life when philosophy began has singular value for the subject. Once philosophy exists, the situation is less unique. Then men are confronted with two forms of inner pursuit—religion and philosophy—which do not have to be created but simply adopted, and the adoption can assume the most diverse equations. Incumbent upon the development of our problem is the necessity to diagnose if this religion and philosophy, which coexist, are *sensu stricto* religion and *sensu stricto* philosophy.

The early thinkers, however, were not confronted with a philosophy outside of themselves to which they would be attracted and induced to combine with their religion. Instead they felt a profound need for some as yet nonexistent entity, which subsequently would be the thing to receive the strange appelation—philosophy. What was it that they were seeking? Why did they seek it? Does it make sense to admit that had they remained within the confines of traditional religion they might have striven to discover something as broad as the latter but completely different in content?

The only means of answering these questions is to immerse ourselves in the preserved fragments of those early thinkers and, by gazing into the distance, try to discover the same horizon as it appeared to those writers. For the moment we are not so much concerned with the thesis expressed in those fragments as in the attitude with which those men responded to what they beheld.

8
The Attitude of Parmenides and Heraclitus*

PARMENIDES AND HERACLITUS were probably born around the year 520 B.C.[1] Thus their thought dates to around the year 500. What was the nature of the mental *soil* in which they were implanted? What intellectual trends, what general modes of thought attracted their youthful minds? What then-contemporary trends delineated for them the *adversary?*

No mention of a proper noun appears in Parmenides' work to serve as a guide. He "cites" neither friend nor foe. And that is not accidental. Parmenides poured his ideas into the mold of a solemn poem,[2] which is in keeping with the most characteristic literary genre of the period—the theological-cosmogenic poem of the Orphic mystics. The genre is mystical and tragic in tone, and the language imposed upon it is aloof and mythical. Although it is composed in the first person, this person is abstract: a *youth*—κοῦρος—who for some reason is protected by young goddesses, vague feminine divinities who are perhaps the Muses or the Hours, for they are called "daugh-

* [Title supplied.—*Ed.*]

1. As I formerly indicated, a discussion on the chronological relationship between the lives of both is not relevant here. What is crucial for us—and striking—is that the works of both were simultaneous and occurred around 475.

2. It seems highly improbable to me that the poem had a title, and even more so that it be entitled *On Nature*, as is conventionally held in Sextus Empericus. A much likelier name, if any, would have been *Aletheia*.

ters of the Sun." This vagueness in the lines, this shadowy
spectral quality of the mythological setting evident in
Parmenides, clearly and unquestionably reveals that Parmenides obliquely, coldly, and calculatingly adopted an
"archaic genre" and used it for his pronouncements. Or
to put it another way: Parmenides used the mythological-
mystical poem without any longer believing in it, as a
mere instrument of expression—in short, as a vocabulary.
The defunct beliefs lasted for a long time transformed
into mere words.[3] Mythology, once it is dead, has an
awesome tenacity. While a belief that is not ours remains
alive in others, we take it seriously and grapple with it,
and at the least take care so that what we say is not confused with what its adherents say. When, however, we
regard a belief to be mummified, it becomes merely an
innocuous "manner of speaking." Thus do we calmly
speak about the Orient as a region where things are born,
precisely because no one still believes in the existence of
such a place in cosmic space that specializes in births.

Not only does Parmenides speak about divine maidens,
but of a formidable Goddess who will teach him the
Truth and of a chariot led by the fleetest, no doubt
winged, steeds, driven by the damsels, and who will lead
him like an Amadis of Gaul along the "polyphemus road"
—the "famous path" that enables "the creature who
knows" to travel the entire universe and be left at the
gates of heaven. All of this constitutes a solemn theatrical
wardobe extracted by Parmenides from old trunks to
serve as a disguise precisely because he used it as a disguise. All that we are obliged to explain is why this man
needed a disguise to say what he wished, why he believed it expeditious to feign a religious, mythological

3. We still name a metal "mercury," Madrilenians go for a
stroll to Neptune's fountain, and some hapless souls suffer from
venereal diseases, that is, diseases of Venus.

tone so that the resounding thunder of his ideas might
descend upon us as pathetic outpourings, delivered in a
revelatory, apocalyptic tone via a goddess' lips. Had we
not foolishly disdained "Rhetorics and Poetics," which
studied *general dicendi*—the manner in which things can
be said—we would readily understand the reason why
Parmenides, in great seriousness (everything about Parmenides is terribly serious), rejected didactic prose,
avoided personal comments, and transferred all of his elo-
cution to vaguely religious characters and figures. *It is
a stylistic necessity*. It is not a whim. Style is the distortion
of common language to suit the author's special motives.
The most frequent motive behind stylization is emotion.
It manipulates tepid, ordinary, insipid language, kindling
and sharpening it, making it reverberate and quiver.[4] Not
only does Parmenides reveal his discoveries but—with a
justification soon to be apparent to us—he is dazzled by
them, he is so overcome with exalted emotion that they
acquire a mystical value for him. If one believes that men
are endowed with airtight compartments, nothing human
will be understood. It is naïve to believe that because a
science may be cold, a frigid truth, that its discovery
lacks the mystical element, that it is not fervid, impassioned, and passionate. And yet, it has been, is, and will

4. At other times when the emotion is of a different sort, wary
and timorous, stylization obtains the opposite effect; it further
decapitates normal language, it renders it even more inexpressive—
for example, in diplomatic language everything is evasive, the
euphemism strongly supplants intuitive expression with fuzzy,
watered-down language. Bear in mind that these distortions of
normal language, which we call "stylizations," are not, at any given
moment, infinite but constitute an available or potential repertory
(one already invented or which the individual can invent for
the occasion) of limited casuistry. To define the forms of stylization is not, therefore, a pointless task—attempting to fence in
the countryside, so to speak. In addition to the grammar of
normal speech, there is need to compose an ultra-grammar of
stylization.

inevitably and happily be that way always. Every "scientific" *discovery*—that is, every truth—suddenly confronts us with an immediate vision of the world, hitherto unperceived and hence not taken into account. Abruptly, as though a veil were removed, it becomes marvelously evident to us—we become "visionaries"—and in addition feel as though we have been overcome by some strange power and uprooted from our habitual "bourgeois" and totally unmystical world into another one—we fall into ecstacy or "rapture." Irrespective of our prior convictions concerning the real and the divine, the commonplace and the magical, the situation—the manner in which the mystical experience is reproduced—is analogous. Descartes, the innovator of the most radical "pure reason," "pure rationalism"—a rationalism summoned to strangulate religion—discovered suddenly when very young, the *method* (from the *"mathesis universalis"*) whereupon he experienced an ecstatic vision that he always regarded as the culminating moment of his life and as something in which he barely had a role, a divine gift, a transcendental revelation. Shaken by that peculiar, unabashed emotion typical of "discoverers," which is infinite humility, he inscribed in his personal notes: *"X novembris 1619, cum plenus forem. Enthousiasmo, et mirabilis scientiae fundamenta reperirem."**

Parmenides regarded the experience of his discovery as, in a sense, a transcendental phenomenon and hence he was most naturally led to employ a religious vocabulary and imagery in order to express simultaneously his idea and his emotion. And this he did precisely because he was not fearful that his readers would take his mystical utterances literally. Hence not only does Parmenides' style indicate

---

* ["10 November 1619, when I was full of enthusiasm, and I discovered the fundamental principles of a wonderful knowledge."]

that he did not believe in the gods, but that likewise amongst the social group whom he addressed, religious faith no longer existed. For Parmenides, the ultimate rationalist, to talk in terms of gods and of celestial excursions, and to employ unwieldly images represents something extraordinary and feverish, which serves to satisfy his need to express felt emotion. A genuine believer, however, would find Parmenides' pen palid, tepid, and coldly allegorical. Anaximander, eighty years earlier, had invented prose and composed his exposition of physics in it. This early prose had not yet been consolidated into a "literary genre," for it was still unsure of itself, that is, of being prose and only prose. When least expected, an emotive, almost mythological gale would sweep over Anaximander's "positivist" language, ruffling the prosaic idiom and imbuing it with visionary flashes. Hence Parmenides had no choice. This explains why he resorted to that fusty mechanism, the *deus ex machina*.

Heraclitus, on the other hand, cited names. He did not dodge the issue. He demanded that Homer and Archilochus be reprimanded (frag. 12). He called the master Hesiod ignorant and unaware of the difference between night and day (frag. 57), he accused Pythagoras of being a charlatan (frag. 129, dubious), and charged Hesiod, Xenophanes, and Hacataeus with concealing their ignorance regarding the only thing worth knowing behind a hodgepodge of ideas (frag. 40). The only puppet not beheaded was Thales, and of him he said: "He was the first astronomer." One hair left on the wolf! The absence of any barbed insult indicates a positive attitude on his part toward Thales and what the latter represented. Noteworthy is the fact that all those cited by name were deceased. Names of contemporaries are missing. One must bear in mind that the most important characteristic intellectual output of the sixth century emanated from the region that included Ephesus, the Ionic coast, and adjacent islands.

Unlike Parmenides, Heraclitus speaks from his own untransferable individuality. His pronouncements, which have baffled so many, and seem so utterly "enigmatic," flash forth like lightning from a mighty, highly individualistic I, from this concrete noninterchangeable man Heraclitus, born of the city's founding family, the Codridas, endowed with "royal" status, in the highest sense of the word, that is, his blood contained the inalienable, divine heritage of "charisma." Heraclitus relinquished the exercise of this divine sovereignty to his brother because even it prevented him from being an absolute individual, the highly unique Heraclitus he felt himself to be.

Before stating what this eminent person said, a brief pause is in order to analyze the manner in which he said it, the formal pattern of his language. Here is what one finds: Parmenides, though emanating from a distinguished family and endowed with the monumental self-confidence typical of the early thinkers—inspired both by consciousness of their existence and of their thought, their aristocratic heritage and their original thinking—imposed respect everywhere by his mere presence. The aura of that respectability appears even in Plato. In the final analysis, however, he mingled among men, he argued with them—his school initiated "discussion," dialectics, as a way of life, striving to convince, not only to demonstrate, but attempting to prove. Parmenides was not distant. Hence in his work he had to create distance and to allow his doctrine to pour forth from the veracious lips of a truthful goddess. Heraclitus, on the other hand, the "king," felt a sense of uniqueness and of unmitigated distance. He retired, as I noted before, from public life, renouncing his sacred magistracy. He felt electrifying contempt for the masses of his fellow citizens and considered them in-

capable of salvation because they did not possess man's
fundamental virtue, which consists in the capacity to recognize superiority.[5] Thus Heraclitus returned from the
public square to the solitary temple of Artemis. Later
he found this to be inadequate and he retired to the innermost depths of a rugged mountain, akin to the merging
of iron and diamonds, within the bowels of the earth.
Rarely has a man possessed a more unlimited conviction
of his superiority over others. *We shall soon see, however,
the underlying inverse reason:* We shall see the utter
humility from which this absolute arrogance sprang and
derived its nourishment. Had Heraclitus still believed in
gods, he would have believed himself a God. Hence he
did not transpose his opinions, projecting them into some
worthier mouth. He did not have to add stylistic distance
to his own distance. His doctrine explains why he felt like
a God—as, in principle, he believed any man had the
right to feel, provided he were not as foolish as men are
wont to be.

One must further bear in mind that in Ionia, where
new thinking and "modern" life originated, the advance
was even greater than that at the other end of Hellas in
Magna Graeca and Sicily. The mythological distance was
greater and prose—the Roman paladin, simple didactic
expression without melodramatism or scenography—had
been solidified. Forty years before, not far from Ephesus,
Hecataeus had written his books on geography and history in pure didactic prose, prose as prosaic and direct as
any to be found in a modern German *Handbuch*.[6] Nevertheless, it was prose that was still inadequate for expound-
ing the strange, transcendental thought that was to be

5. An absurd defect, since in mankind it transpires amongst
those who are simply a wretched flock in need of a shepherd
(see frag. 11).

6. Which does not prevent his prose from occasionally rippling
poetically in *Asianic* flourishes.

philosophy.[7] Thus Heraclitus *could not* write a continuous text book. He expressed his ideas in spurts, in brief pronouncements, which in their attempt each time to be total statements, were stylistically "compressed" and a sort of doctrinal dynamite. Hence his renowned "obscurity." Heraclitus' style therefore consists in expressing his highly individualistic being in the form of thundering pronouncements of the sort that can spout forth in any biting, "flashing," electric conversation. They are maxims, "slang expressions," and yet they have a certain tone which reveals that Heraclitus was influenced by a *genus dicendi* very much in vogue at the time, one with a religious transcendental overtone. This was none other than the oracular and sibylline formulae. He himself in two preserved "fragments" explained why he chose the literary genre of maxims. Granted his conviction that a thinker should devote his thought to universal reason and not be a recondite wizard dedicated to thought, he found the most suitable vehicle to be *similar* to oracular and sibylline divinations. Frag. 92: "The Sibyl who in a delirium utters things unjokingly, unadorned, and unperfumed, reaches milleniums with her voice, for she is divinely inspired." Frag. 93: "The Lord, to whom the oracle of Delphis belongs, neither affirms nor conceals, but suggests." Clearly—at that venerable, creative threshold of philosophy—"suggestion" was being propounded as philosophy's most suitable *vehicle of expression*. What this entails precisely will occupy us at a later point. These

7. Perhaps it is further noteworthy that there has never been a *genus dicendi* truly adequate as a vehicle for philosophizing. Aristotle was unable to resolve this problem that fools ignore. His work has been preserved because he held on to his own lesson notes. I personally have had to contain myself for thirty years while fools accuse me of producing only literature, and the worst part is that even my own students find it necessary to pose the question of whether I have been writing literature or philosophy, along with other ridiculous provincial notions of this order!

two statements of Heraclitus should, however, be interpreted as emanating from a man radically hostile to traditional religion, to the "mysteries," and the "cults."[8] His discoveries nonetheless were *experienced* along with an aspect of revelation, and the mystical impact of this experience found its natural expression in sentences quivering with quasi-religious emotion.

The foregoing stylistic observations pertaining to Parmenides and to Heraclitus could scarcely have been omitted, for they provide the underlying tone of all their statements, as will soon be concretely illustrated. A keen understanding of style is, in this instance, of prime importance. Since we possess but a few fragments of their work and sparse information regarding the period, we cannot neglect what unwittingly is interwoven in their style. In fact our realization that mythology had degenerated for them into mere vocabulary, a *modus dicendi*, is more conclusive than had they themselves stated that mythology, traditional religion, and everything connected with it represented for them the terminated past, something that had descended beyond their vital horizon. Heraclitus' violent attacks against the cult of the gods—the idols—were directed toward the popular segments of society in which archaic faith still persisted. He and Parmenides, however, were combating newer purely mythological forms of "religion," which were not the traditional ones, and as we shall soon see, *appeared on the scene at the same time as the new mode of thought that engaged Parmenides and Heraclitus:* Orphic theology and the "Dionysian mysteries." Mythology, the traditional religion of the Greek city, by then constituted a subsoil for both thinkers. They were not preoccupied or mentally involved with it; it was simply an old verbal usage, automatic and habitual, such as others comprised by lan-

8. See fragments 5, 14, and 15.

guage. Hence it did not matter, if a sentence called for it, to fall back upon the Erinyes, and even less so, to refer to Dike. Nevertheless, Heraclitus made it plainly evident that believers in traditional religion "haven't the slightest notion of what Gods and Heroes really are" (frag. 5).

Heraclitus' *soil* is composed of the intellectual trend that had emerged a century before throughout Greece, particularly in its purest and most pronounced form in Thales of Miletus, in whom it first appeared. In short, what was referred to as Ionian *natural science*. Let us seize the bull by the horns, that is, the one we had in our fingers a moment ago. The only individuals mentioned by Heraclitus without any appended insult are Bias and Thales. And all that he said about the latter was that he was the first astronomer. Heraclitus therefore respected the mode of thinking initiated by Thales, *but* he made it clear that in comparison with his own knowledge, that of Thales and his followers was specialists' knowledge, *nothing more* than astronomy. In order to understand this completely and to diagnose completely, or adequately, the actual *soil* in which both proto-philosophers were implanted, one must recall that Thales flourished around the year 584. It is necessary, therefore, to picture with a certain clarity the profound change that in rapid expansion and accelerated development occurred in Greek life around the year 600 until 500, the date when the work of both proto-philosophers began.

Not only does each of us inhabit a spatial landscape but also a temporal one, with its three dimensions of past, present, and future. Let us for the moment ignore the latter. A certain horizon of the past extends into our own present, it persists, it forms part of the structure of our lives and is an instrument therein. Like every landscape, the past when viewed has perspective, close and distant planes. Each one of these temporal planes acts differently upon our existence. In order to understand a man well one must depict with some precision the chronological topography of his horizon.

The names cited by Heraclitus allow us to reconstruct with considerable clarity the perspective he had of events of Greece's past up to his own day. And with slight modification—due to the fact that the settlements of the west were somewhat less "advanced" than those of the east—the picture serves Parmenides.

In one fragment (42), Heraclitus mentioned Homer and Archilochus together. In another—and in this order—Hesiod, Pythagoras, Xenophanes, and Hecataeus (40). Note that the order in which these names were cited corresponds exactly to historical chronology. Heraclitus' outbursts were written around 475. Hecataeus, the closest to Heraclitus, died when the latter was around twenty years old. Xenophanes, who was a few years older than Hecataeus and Pythagoras, was probably born around 572. These three men therefore "were around" when Heraclitus' life began. Behind them in the intangible distance loomed a character utterly of the past, Hesiod, who composed his *Theogony* around the year 700. Fifty years earlier there was Homer and fifty years later, Archilochus. Thus they were respectively a century and a half, two centuries, and two and a half centuries removed from the youthful Heraclitus—500 B.C. According to Greek temporal optics prior to Aristotle, a century and a half is not a precise time, but rather some hazy, indiscernible, pure "antiquity." Accordingly, Homer and Hesiod are neither more nor less distant than Archilochus. Note that fragment 40 is like a diptych: on the one side Hesiod, and together on the other Pythagoras, Xenophanes, and Hecataeus. In fragment 42 Homer is paired with Archilochus. Hesiod therefore represents the converging point of both groups of names: those completely "ancient" and those completely "modern." They represent for Heraclitus the two great terminal points of the past.

In addition to this *nominative* past, which lies foreshortened in these fragments, is the impersonal one previously discerned in other vituperative fragments—to wit, the religious past. This too is divided into two terminal points of perspective: religious "antiquity," which with the tenacity characteristic of all things religious, survives amongst the people, namely the Homeric and pre-Homeric mythological tradition, the ancient popular gods and the gods of the city. In addition, there existed a "modern" religious past, which was in great vogue among the intermediary social groups: the Dionysian and Orphic mysteries. Around the year 600 both of these began innundating the Greek world.[9]

Orphism, particularly, *culminated around 550* in a form that was completely new for Greece: theology. Mythological religion had always been direct. It did not inspire creation of this secondary form of religion, which consists in speculation on the primary form—that is, theology. Mythology by its very nature is ingenuous, whereas theology is everything except ingenuous. In 550, Pherecydes of Syros composed his theology, which was preceded and followed by others under the legendary names of Epimenides and Onomacrito. One must bear in mind that Orphism and its theologies were ranking intellectual phenomena in Greek at the time that Parmenides and Heraclitus began writing, and that *Pherecydes is a contemporary of Anaximander and belongs to the generation immediately preceding Pythagoras'*.[10]

9. The pre-history of the Dionysian cult is obscure. No one knows when or how this God of Thrace diverged so completely from the Hellenic sphere. The fact is, however, that it did not become an historic force until the year 600.

10. Do not forget that according to my historiological conception, generations are very brief units of time—fifteen years—and

The fact remains, however, that this great mass of the intellectual past, both "ancient" and "modern," personal and impersonal, was completely negated by Heraclitus and Parmenides. They opposed it all, though this opposition was twofold. With regard to traditional religion and "poetry" (Homer, Archilochus) Heraclitus' attitude was summary. He did not seriously contest it since he realized that it no longer existed as a *belief* among any of the alert people of his day. It survived only among the "common people." On the other hand, when it came to the "modern," he adopted a boxer's stance. Proof of this varied response is obvious and abundant. Whereas he devoted only a few random remarks to the gods, the idol cult, and to Homer and Archilochus in scattered fragments, his battle against the "moderns" integrally constitutes all of his doctrine. This difference is confirmed if we examine Parmenides. Since the latter, however, did not cite names, his work lacks incidental attacks. *Thus Parmenides gives no indication of a battle against "antiquity."* Thales—as we shall see—had to overcome the prevailing mythology and he constantly confronted it; Parmenides did not touch upon it.

On the other hand, Parmenides' doctrine, like that of Heraclitus, was a constitutive and formal attack upon the "modern." It is important to distinguish between superfluous, *coincidental attacks,* apparent attacks against an

---

their most important historical characteristic is not—contrary to the usual, old genealogy—to succeed one another, but on the contrary, to overlap. There are always *three* "contemporary" generations and the equation of their triple dynamism constitutes the *concrete reality* of every historical date. It is well to recall that it was I who relaunched—and this time seriously—the *decisive* theme of generations. See Pinder, *Das Problem der Generation,* 1928, Prologue. The exposition of my concrete doctrine of generations did not emanate from knowledge of Pinder. The complete formularization was presented in the course on Galileo in the Valdecilla Chair, 1933. [*Man and Crisis, Complete Works,* Vol. V.]

obviously definite enemy, and *constitutive attacks* that are integral to a theory. Xenophanes provides a further example and datum illustrative of the demise of Greek "antiquity" and the fact that within a few years it no longer existed upon the *contemporary horizon* even as an adversary. Xenophanes was probably born in 565, hence a half century before Heraclitus and Parmenides. The existing fragments of his poems reveal the dauntless, head-on battle he waged against the gods and Homer, signifying that the latter were *still extant* during his lifetime. They constituted his *adversary*. Half a century later things had changed. The gods and Homer were no longer a burning issue for the elite. They had descended beyond the horizon. The new *adversary* consisted, on the one hand, of new forms of religion, which were occupying the position formerly held by the undisputed empire of ancient mythology and Homerism, and on the other hand, of new forms of a nonreligious and even antireligious category—in short, of a "scientific" nature—which both men found radically inadequate. One must carefully demark the plane that both of these phenomena occupied for the thinker born in the last twenty years of the sixth century, or else he will be unable to perceive with total clarity the significance of the utterly astonishing mental agitation evident in the writings of Parmenides and Heraclitus.

The fact remains however that up to now the text of these two men reveals only a *negative* past. Did they have total disrespect for the entire intellectual past? There is no doubt that they were two giants of discontent, two fabulous heroes of contempt. Parmenides' poem, despite its solemnity and hieratism, bristles throughout with insults, and there is hardly a line imprinted in Heraclitus that does not discharge a verbal blow. The reason for this ferocity will soon emerge. Let us baldly state, though, that both men were blind to all compromise and that their ideas emerged with unparalleled radicalism.

Heraclitus, however, did evince symptoms of a *positive* past. As noted, praiseworthy mention was given by him to Bias of Priene and Thales of Miletus. The latter were two of the "Seven Wise Men."[11] Thales, the oldest of the Seven, was always considered the most prominent. Without attempting here to divine what comprised the Wise Men's "wisdom," let us suggest only two of its attributes. One: the Seven Wise Men's wisdom constituted the first secularized knowledge, removed in theme and method from the preceding religious-poetic tradition. Furthermore, it represented knowledge that emanated directly from individuals. Prior to that, everything with any claim to "wisdom" was impersonal in nature. The individual's role was that of a substratum for expressing wisdom that he could not claim to have derived personally. One of the essential qualities, however, of the wisdom of the Seven Wise Men was that it originated in one particular eminent individual. For reasons soon to be made evident, a Wise Man was there to vouch for the wisdom and not the reverse: he was the tree to recommend the fruit.

Although an exploration of the content of this "knowledge" will not be undertaken here, a simple reading of the representative names reveals two strata. There was, firstly, the "wisdom" common to them all, but in addition to this there were more specialized forms of individual creation initiated or at least elucidated by particular individuals. In fact, Thales was not only one of the Seven Wise Men, but as Heraclitus himself notes, he was the "first astronomer," that is, the innovator of *physiology* or Ionian *physics*—the first "scientific" thinker to exist in the

11. As is known, there existed various lists of "wise men" that differed numerically and by the inclusion of like names. The reduced "seven" first appeared in Plato.

world. Periander was the *first* tyrant. "Tyranny" and "science" were contemporary inventions. Solon was the legislator of Athens. The year 600 likewise marked the innovation of legislation that stemmed from one individual and of the literary genre of "law writing."[12] In fact, the only thing in this human world, apart from reason, considered worthy by Heraclitus was law, and to be more precise, law created by man.

Thus Heraclitus' "positive past" was not meager, since Ionian philosophy and its derivations—tyranny and legislation—constitute two thirds of the "modernity" that informed Greek intellectual life between 600 and 500 B.C.

If we balance things now, we find that the *soil* inhabited by Parmenides and Heraclitus was formed by a strange convolution of intellectual initiatives, which like an eruption suddenly broke the "traditional" crust of Greek life in the year 600. This convolution was composed of the following elements: the Dionysian mysteries, Orphism, proto-geography and proto-history, Ionian physics, arithmetic, Pythagorian ethics and mysticism, tyranny and legislation. Part of that *soil* became the adversary for Parmenides and Heraclitus, since an *adversary* is always a contemporary, something standing in the same *soil* and holding much in common. One does not combat that which is totally alien.

Our gleaning, however, has merely yielded us an inventory of human forms, heterogeneous in aspect. We must now try to understand them, and we shall understand them only by finding their common root, and in addition, the clue that will enable us to discover beneath their apparent divergence and dispersion their common inspiration. All of them began to flower during the first twenty years of the sixth century. Proto-philosophy is

12. It is known that Plato somewhat ironically regarded written laws as a literary genre.

the fruit produced by that Spring exactly one century afterward, between 500 and 470. We have now made the preparations for attempting the historiological process: the reconstruction of origins.

Every period is understood as emerging from one or a few events, fundamental events, which as it were, are at their core. What Greece was between 600 and 500 is rooted in the following precise event: Around 650 Hellenic colonization reached its last frontiers in all four cardinal directions. The vital tide of Greek national expansion attained its peak.[13] Immediately—and this phenomenon deserves broader consideration—the colonial periphery began to react upon continental and metropolitan Greece. Homer, a typical colonial product, had preceded this by a century.

Greek culture, if we so label what comes to constitute "classicism," as we know it, had long been anticipated by the colonies. Science and philosophy, especially, were originally colonial events. Athens delayed—two centuries! —in creating an indigenous philosophy, and it could never boast of many. Whenever philosophy is discussed, Athens is the first to come to mind. The truth is closer to the contrary, and the question might well be asked if Athens in fact was not a hindrance for philosophy, since its tenacious reactionism consubstantial with its democracy, was responsible for the pathological evolution of Greek thought, which *prevented* it thereby from attaining full maturity. This supposition, however—that Greek thought remained sickly and hence abnormal in development— has the ring of blasphemy not only for Hellenic worshipers, but more generally, for all those who regard historical events per se as something merely to be annotated. The latter approach is historical *positivism*. In

13. The enlargement produced by Alexander's campaigns was an increase in the number of states, rather than one of national change.

my judgment, however, history is a rich repertory of possible operations that ought to be coordinated with events, and these operations begin precisely once the event has been noted. History, as I was saying, signifies not only recounting the past but understanding it, and now I add that if it signifies understanding it, it of necessity likewise means criticizing it, and consequently becoming enthused, anguished, and irritated by it, censuring, applauding, correcting, and completing it, crying and laughing over it. It is not a mere manner of speaking; history taken seriously is integrally a form of life in which the historian involves himself fully, if he is truly a man—partially with his intellect, but also hounded by the entire pack of his passions, *cum ira et studio.*

9

Philosophy and a Period of Freedom

PHILOSOPHY was one fruit, among others, that was born in Greece when its people entered the "period of freedom."

Confining the word "freedom" primarily or exclusively to law and politics, as though these were the root from which the general configuration of human life known as freedom springs, is an error that reduces and flattens the enormity of the subject. The issue is indeed much broader. Freedom is the aspect assumed by a man's whole life when the diverse components in it reach a point in their development to produce among themselves a particular dynamic equation. To have a clear idea of what "freedom" is, presupposes having defined or found with some rigor the formula for that equation.

Probably every civilization or *curriculum vitae* of a related group of people passes through that form of life known as freedom. It is a brief, glowing stage that unfolds like noon between the morning of primitivism and the decline of evening, the petrification and necrosis of its senescence. The categorical stages of a civilization are determined and discerned as modifications of the fundamental relation between the two great components of human life, man's needs and his possibilities.

In the primitive or early stage, man has the impression that his circle of possibilities barely transcends that of his needs. He feels that what man *can* do in his life coincides almost strictly with what he *has* to do. His margin of choice is extremely scant; or to phrase it differently: there is a paucity of things that man can do. Life does not have an aspect of "richness" to him. Note that it is equally incorrect to assign the term "riches" or wealth primarily to the economic realm, as it was to consign the idea of freedom to politics and to law. In both instances, the true relationship consists in the fact that both juridical freedom and economic wealth are, though extremely important and symptomatic, only effects or manifestations of generic freedom and vital wealth. Wealth in the economic sense means simply that man is confronted with numerous possibilities for possession and acquisition, or concretely, with many things to own, buy, and sell. How much or how little must be interpreted in relation to the subjective consciousness that man has of his needs. If one generalizes this concept to all other orders of human existence, besides the economic, the conclusion is as follows: Until a certain date, amongst a particular group of people, individuals of a cultural ambit feel that they can scarcely rely upon any possibilities other than those strictly essential to their needs. Living therefore means relying on what there is and thanking God that there is enough to live! Something to eat, a little knowledge, a little pleasure. Life is poverty. Man lives by utilizing the frugal repertory of intellectual, technical, ritualistic, political, and festive resources laboriously created and accumulated by tradition. Under this sort of equation an individual is never in the position of being able to choose; for choice assumes that the circle of one's possibilities is notably greater than that of one's needs.[1]

1. Note what this means. In actuality, even within this vital equation, the individual now and then is faced with the possibility of choice, but so infrequently does this happen that he is unaware of it and does not regard it as a special function of his life. In order for a mode of life to emerge with particular characteristics

Gradually relations between the members of this historical entity increase, as does intercourse, knowledge, and traffic with its periphery, or with "foreigners." *Life expands*, at least spatially. The world one inhabits is enlarged. Concomitantly, commerce, industry, and the discovery of mines upon remote shores are initiated.[2] Economic wealth appears. Simultaneously, new techniques, arts, and pleasures become abundant. Man experiences life as consisting not solely of what there is but as the creation and extraction of new realities from oneself; hence, life is no longer defined exclusively by its necessities, but overflowing these, it consists in abundant possibilities. The word "abundant" unwittingly is imposed; life is abundance; the term expresses the hyperbolic relationship between possibilities and needs. *There are more things, more possible things, to do (haceres) than are needed.* Luxury, or lust, begins. *Ipso facto* the individual finds that living is a problem totally different from what it was in the archaic stage. Then it meant abiding by what there was and . . . thanking God for it! Resignation, humble gratitude to God for granting the essentials. Now, however, the problem is reversed: one has to choose among many possibilities. Life is symbolized by the cornucopia. One must select. The basic emotion of existence is now the opposite of resignation, for living means "having things in excess." Whereupon the basic emotion of petulance, the superabundance of existence, of "humanism," begins. The realization that new things have been invented becomes

---

and for men to take notice of it, mere existence is not enough. The mode must appear often enough so that it assumes some proportion and conspicuousness.

2. History's "regularity," or one might say monotony, is surprising. The pleonastic period is initiated in Phoenicia and Carthage by the discovery of Spanish mines, in Greece by the mines in Pontus, in Europe by the Portuguese discovery on the African coast of "The Mine" that is still called Elmina.

functionalized and man deliberately begins to invent. *To create a new life* becomes a normal function of life—something that would not have occurred to one during the primitive stage of life. Revolutions begin.

Symptomatically the individual ceased to be totally inscribed to tradition, even though his life was still partially governed by it. Whether he wanted to or not, he was the one to *choose* among the superabundant possibilities. And let us not exclude amongst these the intellectual possibilities. As countries frequented one another, traveled, and became immersed in things exotic, they learned different ways of seeing things, *modi res considerandi*. The individual, instead of being dependent on a single unquestioned repertory of opinions—traditions—was faced with a broad selection and forced to choose by *himself* the one he found most convincing. The possibility and consequent necessity of selecting one's opinion on something was the human experience upon which so-called "rationalism" was based. And to such a degree that unbeknownst perhaps to the reader, we have been able to describe this situation with the same words Aristotle employed centuries later in his definition of science: ἐπιστήμη ἐστὶ ἡ ὑπόληψις ἡ πιστοτάτη (Science is the most persuasive supposition).

Does this reveal clearly what is signified by "vital wealth"? Man's existence—and the world in which it transpired—was enormously enlarged, its contents filled to exuberance. For the first time in civilization, man felt that life was worth the effort of living. At the same time the attitude toward religion changed. Religion always implies transcendence, even in the least transcendent instance, as in Greece. Gods are ultra- or super-worldly powers. Amid a life of poverty the individual needs God so much that his life derives *from* God. Every act, every moment of his existence has reference and connection with the divinity. The very instruments of life are so crude, so innately ineffectual, and in themselves, so much of this world, that man has little faith in their efficacy and has faith only in the *virtue* with which God, through magical rite, infuses them. This means that life itself and this wretched world barely interpose between man and God. As life swelled, however, and the world grew richer, the increasing bulk of the worldly element intervened between man and God, and separated them. Affirmation of this world and of life in it became valid in its own right. Irreligiousness was the result. Just as the aforementioned cause separated men from tradition, so this *surrender to worldly life* uprooted him from religion. All the consequences encumbent upon the former were carried to the extreme: amid a life of abundance man was left uprooted, dangling in mid-air. He floated amid the aerial element of his mounting possibilities. This was the inevitable counterbalance. The stability and vital security of an individual's existence were not automatically and effortlessly bestowed upon him by innate adherence to an unquestioned tradition, but the individual himself with total awareness had to fabricate a foundation, a *terra firma* to support himself. Hence he had no choice; using the fluid, ethereal matter available from existing possibilities, he had to construct for himself a world and a life. Now this implies "rationalizing" simple existence, rather than existing spontaneously, with abandon, without any ado.

When earlier I pointed out that during "periods of freedom" men live upon a foundation of emotional petulance and superabundance, I did not imply thereby the attribute of security. Human life is always insecure, a fact implicit in every equation of it, although each reflects a different aspect. The insecurity of the poor man is one and the insecurity of the rich man another. Thus the insecurity of the "free" prepotent man is extremely curious:

it means not knowing what to do simply because there are so many things to be done, whereupon one has the impression of being lost, of evaporating amid sheer possibilities. A concrete example of this sense of being lost, of shipwreck amid abundance (note that the very word *ab-undancia* retains the image of an inundating, overwhelming torrent), occurs in the realm of thought, that is, of opinions, a symptomatic phenomenon of such periods: namely, doubt. Doubt is not simply nonbelief. Someone who holds no opinion about something is ignorant, but he does not doubt. Doubt presupposes that one is confronted with positive opinions, each of which *might* warrant belief, and precisely for that reason, mutually paralyze their power to convince. Man is *stranded amid* the various opinions, none of which is able to sustain him firmly—hence he slips about amid the many possible "knowledges" and finds himself falling, falling into a strange liquid medium . . . *he falls into a sea of doubts*. Doubt is a fluctuation of opinion, that is, a desperate flailing amid waves—*fluctus*. Hence doubt is a "state of mind" that is not a permanent state, but unstable. Man cannot remain in it. He must *emerge* from doubt and for this he seeks a means. The means by which one emerges from doubt and becomes lodged in firm conviction constitutes the method. Every method is a reaction to a doubt. Every doubt is a postulation of a method. Descartes in his invention of "methodical doubt" provides a superb example of skill and intellectual elegance in combining both elements with utter simplicity.

10

The Historical Origin of the Profession of Philosophy*

WHAT IS the underlying meaning of Thales' assertion: "All things are full of gods"? As in all assertions, someone is saying something to someone; the textual meaning has two dimensions. One consists in what the text appears to be saying. The other is the fact that a particular individual is addressing his statement to another individual or a specific group. Only through integration of both dimensions can the concrete textual meaning be derived.

Let us endeavor to interpret Thales' assertion in its strict textual sense. It would seem to signify that there exist as many gods as things and occurrences, implying thereby the futility of discriminating between things and gods, or more properly still, that there are no things, only gods. Since deities and things are mutually exclusive and since gods pervade everything, then everything must be devoid of things.

Thus it is unlikely that Thales in this context employed the term gods in its usual, direct sense—that of religious tradition—but in some oblique new sense. The primary attribute of gods who were gods *sensu recto* was that of representing the extraordinary in opposition to the ordinary; the privileged, uncommon reality in contrast to daily, habitual reality. At certain points and at certain

* [Title supplied.—*Ed.*]

moments of reality God intervened as a contrast to the rest of reality in which God was not present. The most ancient division in the human mind was between the sacred and the profane. One might say that certain exceptional phenomena, aristocratic in nature, seemed to exist in the world wherein the presence and intervention of God occurred. What meaning can there be in this democratization, this universalization of the divine seemingly proposed by Thales' statement? Evidently that the deities had ceased to represent the exceptional and the extraordinary and had become ubiquitous and commonplace; that is, when Thales made reference to the gods, in his mind they had lost their primary attribute and had ceased to be actual gods, but had been transmuted into mere things, or rather into something residing in each thing that was the principle of its reality and its characteristic modes of behavior. The gods were downgraded into causes.

The enunciation of a geometrical theorem is directed to no one in particular, but to men in general, to the *vernünftiges Wesen* (rational being) whom Kant spoke about with such enthusiasm. This indeterminateness respecting one's interlocutor is evinced by the statement of the theorem, for the latter never alludes to any opinions divergent from its own asserted content. Hence, a theorem never conveys the impression of forming part of a dialogue. Now Thales' foregoing comment has essentially the aspect of dialogue. He is rectifying, correcting a preexistent opinion—to be precise, a "public opinion," or common *doxa*—according to which gods reside only in certain privileged phenomena. In its form of expression, Thales' statement belongs to the epigrammatic style of the Seven Wise Men. The latters' dialogues were held with public opinion or with the other sages. χαλεπὸν ἐσθλὸν ἔμμεναι (It is difficult to be good), Pittacus declared and

Solon replied, χαλεπὰ τα καλά (The beautiful is difficult).[1]

In an excellent article on "faith among the Olympic gods"[2] Bruno Snell says: *"der Gedanke, die Götter könnten vielleicht nicht existieren, hat überhaupt erst um die Mitte des 5. Jaurhunderts geaüssert werden können."* The formula is wary and consequently ambiguous. Note that implicit in it is the assumption that from the sixth century up to that date, atheism had mounted, extended, and intensified among the Greeks. According to Snell, Protagoras was the first one to deny expressly the existence of the gods. Actually, Protagoras only claims that it is impossible to know whether or not gods exist, or granting that they do exist what their forms are, a thesis which is in line with the universality of his skeptical relativism, and therefore loses much of its audacity. Do Protagoras' words signify, however, a more resounding negation of the gods than those of Heraclitus and Xenophanes? Finally, Protagoras did not substitute another reality for the gods, whereas Xenophanes and Heraclitus dislodged the Pantheon and in lieu of the plurality of gods fundamental to Greek religion, they talked about one God whose primary attribute was his oneness. Anaximander did the same thing, and was thereupon regarded as an atheist. The God who appears at the conclusion of an argument is obviously not a religious God, but a theoretical principle. The discoverer no doubt was someone who had abandoned religious belief, and feeling lost in a world whose traditional foundations were severed, felt compelled to seek through intellectual free choice a new foundation. This free choice of principles has been called "rationality."

1. Wilamowitz, *Sapho und Simonides,* p. 174.
2. *Das neue Bild der Antiquen,* I, p. 113, 1942. ("The idea that the gods perhaps did not exist, could be expressed, generally, around the middle of the fifth century.")

If the name philosophy is given to this free choice of principles, it seems indubitable that the creation of philosophy presupposes a stage of atheism. During the sixth century, among certain enclaves in colonial Greece, religion ceased to be a possible way of life and consequently a new position toward the changed existence had to be devised in opposition to religious existence. In no way was this opposition more clearly evident than in the use of the term "god" for entities whose attributes invalidated the "popular gods" of Greek religion. We are informed by Cicero of Antisthenes' statement in his *Physics: Populores Deos multos, naturalem unum esse* (The gods of the people are many, but the god of nature is one alone).[3]

Dating from Greek antiquity, the word "God" was imbued with great semantic mobility. Plutarch in his essay on "How a young man should interpret his reading of the poets" asserted: "One must realize, and never lose sight of the fact, that among poets [reference is made to Homer] the words *Zeus, Zin* at times designate God himself, but at other times Fortune, and often also Fate." (§6) Similarly Cicero, in the first book of *De natura deorum*, acts surprised when he naïvely discovers that philosophers have applied the nouns *theos, theion, daimon,* etc., to the most diverse things, hence, using them contradictorily. Thus he found that in Aristotle, God represents understanding as well as the stars in their incessant revolution. On reading *Timaeus* we are surprised by the repeated rectification Plato feels compelled to make when mentioning the "Gods" in this dialogue. At first he employed the word in its full religious sense, but forthwith realized that the word then did not make sense since the gods were no more than stars and the earth as such a sidereal body. He was thereby obliged to correct himself and to

3. *De natura deorem*, I, XIII.

use the term "Gods" in its physical sense. Note the clear distinction and even derision in the double meaning whereupon he distinguished between "the revolving or orbicular gods and those which appear when they feel like."[4] This indicates that the terms still lacked a specific character of reality, which would have to be delineated and which would not admit of contradictions, but that they had become instead titles of ontological nobility bestowable upon the most diverse entities. Burnet suggests that this ambiguous use of the term God by the philosophers—as evinced in Aristophanes' *The Clouds*—was the cause of the violent reaction aroused against them by Athenian public opinion.

More, however, than in any pronouncement patently denying the existence of religious gods, the atheism of Ionian natural science was manifest in the mode of thought that engendered it. This mode of thought represented the complete inversion of the mythical *logos* from which the gods originated. Human reality, the "habitual World" thereby was characterized by a limited, accidental, and ominous potentiality. This experience of human impotence—life itself—constituted a mental blow and compelled one through "dialectical necessity" to devise another inherently different reality: one of unlimited potentiality, free from chance, and self-assured. This reality was "the divine," the *numenous* substance out of which were carved particular, specialized powers and gods, from ephemeral deities to God in detailed biography.

Thus, the mythical *logos*, in order to "explain" or establish human reality, which is *present* reality, imagined some other prior reality in an absolute *before* or *alcheringa*, in the terminology of Australian aborigines, created precisely because in that prior reality things were pos-

4. *Tim.*, 40d–41a.

sible that were not possible in the human present. Ionian thought—not only among the natural scientists but equally in Hecataeus—attempted inversely to explain the *before*—the origin of things, the *physis*—by constructing it in accordance with the experimental law of our lives. Hence the present explains the past, which thus explained, becomes an effective *before*, a past united in continuity with the present, surviving in it, and thereby serving as a permanent foundation. Consequently Hecataeus introduced historical *theory* as an intellectual *construction* of the past *by means of* the present. Traditional opinion was invalidated, stigmatized as humbug, and in contraposition the new opinion emerged as the solid one—that is, the true one. Thus it is seemingly essential to truth that it emerge upon a background of errors recognized as such.

The onset of a mode of thought that so radically inverts traditional thought and transforms the world into an inherently profane reality, does not seem possible unless we imagine the early thinkers as being utterly devoid of religious faith. It is neither necessary nor accurate to assume an intensification of atheism during the fifth century. More astonishing than commonly regarded, is the fact that not a single text appeared among the Ionian natural scientists in which the slightest role was attributed to the traditional gods. Hence Thales' assertion ought not to be interpreted in the sense that his ubiquitous gods are "divine" in nature, but exactly the opposite. The statement is mildly ironic and euphemistic in character.

Important to note is the radical stylistic difference between the Ionian natural scientists and the founding philosophical thinkers—Heraclitus, Parmenides, and Xenophanes. The former calmly expounded their opinions, whereas the latter angrily reared up against the populace and heaved insults upon their predecessors either nominatively or generically. So evident is this that the absence

of a study of it is surprising. Why did philosophy begin
with an onrush of invective? A good deal of time had
elapsed between the Ionians and Heraclitus. The death
of Anaximenes, who was the last of the Ionians, probably
coincided with the birth of Heraclitus. This means that
a new type of man was probably in the forming during
the fifth century: the "thinker." The vagueness of the
word was befitting, since the reality thereby designated
was also vague. The thinker as such was not to exist for
another century and then in Plato's Academy—if one is
willing to concede that the thinker's existence has ever
been truly possible in history, our own times included.
Heraclitus' and Parmenides' generation found this new
human figure, typified both in character and profession,
already formed, though hazy. The first practitioners of
this occupation, whose practice consisted in *theory*, were
incapable yet of regarding themselves as thinkers, just as
Julius Caesar could not see himself as a caesar. Their
occupation was an individual's concrete thing to do. The
occupation had to be practiced by a series of individuals
before it became not an individual concern but something
typical, delineating a *type* of person, and endowed with
the markings of a trade or magistracy. Hence the change
in style. Heraclitus, despite his hypertrophic individuality,
speaks as a *magistrate of thought*. Obviously they were
not yet addressing themselves to the common people, for
the latter did not yet have the slightest inkling about this
type of individual. They addressed themselves to certain
minority groups who were informed on particular intellectual currents of the time, who discussed Homer and
Hesiod and were acquainted with Orphic theology, yet
finally adhered to traditional opinions. For Heraclitus and
Parmenides, these groups represented the populace, and
they were the butt of part of their indignities. In a way,
insulting the populace is the thinker's characteristic tenor,

for his mission, his professional destiny, is to possess his "own" ideas, in opposition to the *doxa* or public opinion. If one were merely seeking for agreement, a new magistracy would be unnecessary. Hence Heraclitus and Parmenides were completely aware that in confronting and opposing the *doxa*, their opinion was constitutively *paradoxa*. This paradoxical character has prevailed throughout all of philosophy's evolution. Similarly, Amos, the first Hebrew "thinker" and a contemporary of Thales, made it evident that when God chose him for his profession, God imposed this mandate upon him: "Prophesy *against* my people."[5] Every prophet is a prophet *against*, as is every "thinker." In the course of Plato's work, where he speaks most concretely about the early "thinkers," he expressly emphasizes the paradoxical, and hence abstruse, pattern of their thought, saying: "Their lack of concern toward us reveals their uncommon contempt for common men, and never worrying about whether we are able to follow them or not, they each unperturbedly conclude what they have to say."[6]

Although the "thinker" by the beginning of the fifth century already had a sense of self-awareness in his role as such, and realized that he was performing an important function, one with a special mission and the status of a magistracy, his professional guise was not yet sufficiently consolidated for the populace, the genuine populace, to perceive it and for him to assume a stance. Hence the incomparable freedom that the Ionian natural scientists enjoyed as the first philosophers. The "thinker" was still not a social figure.

The socialization of the "thinker" came about during the fifth century. But with respect to this subject, our incongruent information tends to grossly distort Greek

5. Amos VII, 15.
6. Soph., 243 A.

history. Although we have substantial data on Athens, we know very little about the other cities. About Sparta itself, despite its historical stature, our information is so scant that we are unable even to picture its daily life. Sparta however could be overlooked in this context, inasmuch as we are dealing with events pertaining to the first philosophers. We cannot however do likewise with other cities, since it was there and not in Athens where the "thinkers" were born and lived during the first half of the fifth century. It was in them and not in Athens that this new type of individual was formed. What was the relation between him and the city he dwelled in? It is impossible for us to formulate a notion of this. Our grounds are only meager for suspecting that it differed considerably from the relationship that existed between the "thinker" and Athens from the fourth century on. It is impossible, given our scant data, to interpret otherwise the fact that most of this data consists in revealing the philosopher in his displacement from one city to another or else intervening in political struggles. This contrasts with the predominant stability of philosophers in Athens after 400.

We suffer therefore from a blindness of sixty years, precisely the period during which the "thinker" as a social figure took form. We owe this blindness to the fact that Athens, the only city that stands brightly illumined for us in terms of information, was backward in relation to the periphery of the Greek world insofar as "thought" was concerned. On the periphery, theories had been developing for a century and a half, whereas no "thinker" emerged amongst the Athenians. Pericles, with the snobbism befitting a good aristocrat, had to send for Anaxagoras around 460. Shortly afterward, around 440, we enjoy full visibility and the "thinker" appears as a social figure, that is, as a new type of individual perceived and recognized as such by the *demos*. This does not imply that their view of him was adequate. It could not be.

For a "people" as profoundly reactionary and intensely adherent to traditional beliefs, it was an extremely unsettling experience. Their "intellectual" backwardness, which coincided with their political triumph over Greece and their sudden fabulous surge in wealth, meant that everything that had been fermenting in Hellas for a century and a half, landed at one fell sweep upon the plazas and porticos of Athens. Side by side with traditional poetry and *mitopeia*, the Athenian public for the first time was abruptly presented with a variegated bountifulness of the new products of the mind. Sophists came from the East and delivered stylized speeches; they publicized their "thinkers" (according to Aristophanes); they expounded the new Ionian, Pythagorean, Eleatic science; they offered the spectacle of extracting models of geometric bodies and armillary spheres from their boxes; they explained ellipses with facts of the utmost simplicity and devoid of all mystery. Meanwhile, the "sophist" Herodotus recounted exotic histories to the Greeks; he described other lands and other peoples and what had happened in them and to them. An avalanche of "paradoxas" besieged Athens. Rumored about was the terrible blasphemy that the stars were not deities but balls of burning metal, like the Sun, for example, which according to Anaxagoras was bigger than Peloponnesus.[7]

This was the first time that the confrontation of the "thinker" and populace was witnessed. It was inevitable that people lost their bearings amid such chaotic innovation and were unable to distinguish between the assorted professions represented therein. Even elite groups such as the poets were unable to grasp the distinction clearly. In this early phase the "thinker" as a social figure invariably

7. See Wilanowitz, *Plato,* I, p. 65 ss.

appears in sketchy profile. This alone can explain the extravagant appearance attributed by Aristophanes to Socrates in *The Clouds*. It is a matter upon which philosophers have shown the least perspicacity. Its solution requires that one begin with the assumption that Aristophanes knew what Socrates was, but that he was inspired by the comic muse to distort what he beheld. It is pathetic to view the efforts made by philologists to exonerate the poet for this distortion as if in any event one could logically expect to find in *The Clouds* a congruent portrait of the philosopher. It is pointless in this instance to dwell specifically on distortion, for it is self-evident. Every distortion reveals its orientation and the initial form of the object that has been exaggerated and decomposed. In *The Clouds* the initial form is clearly revealed and one recognizes that it did not depict Socrates the individual but some vague figure whom Aristophanes and most Athenians of the day conceived of as the "thinker." Note that the most prominent feature of that caricature was one in actuality furthest removed from the real Socrates, namely an interest in "meteorology," in celestian phenomena.

One thing however is certain: a particular type of individual did emerge as a social figure and was reacted to by society. In fact, no sooner did Anaxagoras, the first philosopher, arrive in Athens, than the Athenian populace began reacting with an unparalleled sentiment of uneasiness. The Greeks found a word in their language to categorize the varieties of human conduct that elicited this displeasure: they called it περιττός (excessive). Aristotle explicitly relates that the populace criticized men like Anaxagoras and Thales because the latter busied themselves with περιττά (extravagances).[8] The word does not translate readily into our tongues because of its numerous semantic overtones. On the one hand it signifies

8. Eth. Nik. 1141 b, 3.

an extraordinary act or work of laudatory value, and on the other it denotes excessive, extravagant, and particularly in the religious sense, improper and hence sacrilegious conduct. Pedro Simon Abril, a sixteenth-century Spanish humanist, and a translator of the *Ethics*, translated περιττά in this passage as "knowing too much." To my mind that is the closest translation.[9]

As soon as the populace became aware of the "thinker" as a figure, the latter's position altered radically, for the social reaction was negative and the thinker in his action had to resort to certain precautionary defenses. The religious attitude prevailed with full force among the Athenian populace. This conviction included the belief that certain earthly secrets existed which warranted the respect of mortals, inasmuch as any knowledge of them was the privilege of the gods. Hence, Athenians believed that all attempts to scrutinize these secrets were tantamount to disbelief in the gods. Everything that transpired in heaven was divine. Hence "meteorology," which sought to fathom celestial secrets, their origin, nature, and pattern of behavior, appeared as a blasphemous endeavor. The ire of the *demos* could not be forestalled. And in fact, in the last third of the sixth century, the three most prominent philosophers in Athens—Anaxagoras, Protagoras, and Socrates—were either exiled, or as in the case of the latter, "liquidated."

We see in the reaction of the Athenian people macroscopic confirmation that atheism was a basis for the new profession initiated by the Ionians. The two forms of life were from the start antagonistic and incompatible.

The "thinker's" new and difficult public position provided the origin of the name "philosophy," a name that is

9. Lasson mis-translates, for the passage must be interpreted in relation to 1177 b, 33.

strange, affected, and inexpressive. It is interesting to
observe, though, at how early a date "thinkers" were concerned with what their profession should be called. In
Plato a page and a half is devoted to Protagoras tackling
this problem. It is revealed that the word "sophist" was
an ancient one and applicable to poets, musicians, and
soothsayers, but that once it became discredited and con-
ducive to arousing people's animosity, an attempt was
made to avoid it and to find substitutes. Plato would have
us believe that the word "sophist" is valid as he understood it, although for the masses it meant the vague con-
glomeration of all the exponents of the new opinions.
Significant for us in the present context is that Plato
described the "thinker's" position in the face of public
opinion as a perilous one.

The "thinker" had to conceal the profession to which
he was dedicated by eschewing its revelatory name and
resorting to disguises and precautions, or πρόσχημα
ποιεῖσθαι καὶ προκαλύπτεσθαι εὐλάβεια.[10] Time and again
Plato alludes to the hostility encountered by the philosopher in his social milieu, and even at the end of his life,
in the *Laws*—821A—Plato found it necessary to protest
that scientific inquiries, especially those of an astronomical
and philosophical nature, were of an impious nature—
οἱ σοφοί. So tenacious was this public attitude that even
Alexander of Aphrodesia explicitly labeled περιττοί (wise
men) as περιττοὺς (excessive).[11]

It is curious that never during this initial stage in
"thought" was the name *sophoi* applied to its practitioners even by themselves. The word was an ancient one.
It has an exact correspondent in the Latin *sapiens*, and its
root is Indo-European. Homologous expressions existed
among the most primitive people to designate what per-

10. Prot. 316 d, 317 b.
11. Comm. in Met. 529 (982 b 29, 983 a. 2).

haps constituted the oldest profession of mankind: a man, generally an elder, entrusted with tasting foods to distinguish between those which were salutary for the tribe, hence a sampler of plants in particular and a connoisseur of tastes or savors, *sapores.* Plants savor of something, *sapor,* due to their juice—in Germanic *Saft;* they are *sapient.* The term transfers from the object to the subject "one who understands savors"—the *sapiens,* the *sophos.* This was probably the original Sisyphean meaning. This meaning, however, extended to all dimensions of human life, among them all the technical ones, always referring, however, to a nontheoretical, still nonexistent type of knowledge. The "knowledgeable" individual understands certain things not because he possesses general ideas (theories) about them, but because he lives in perpetual, concrete contact with them, and is aware of their simultaneous individuality and their immense variety and casuistry. Hence—someone who "understands" porcelain or "antiques." It is an empirical and barely transferable knowledge. Now, of all things worth understanding, is human life itself, both personal and collective. The content of this knowledge pertaining to the structure of human life and its vicissitudes was called "wisdom" and it forms the "wisdom literature." The ancient word *sophos* thereupon suddenly acquired a more precise connotation referring to the Seven Wise Men, who were all men of state. The best example of the content of their knowledge exists in Solon's *Elegies.* Compare these with the fragments of the "natural scientists" or of the protophilosophers Parmenides and Heraclitus. Solon was occupied only with human life and he did not theorize. His doctrine of the seven ages exudes vital experience.

The concept of the Seven Wise Men, their utterances, and their legend attained such popularity in Greece that the name *sophos* became inadequate to designate the new "thinkers." A more up-to-date, less prestigious, and more modest word had to be found: *sophistes*. Whereas *sophos* directly designates the man himself as being wise, sophist denominates him professionally, be it in poetry, music, the art of divination, etc. Since the work of the "thinkers"—not only "natural scientists" and philosophers, but grammarians, rhetoricians, travelers, etc.—meanwhile had become consolidated into a body of "wisdoms," the acquisition of which necessitated an apprenticeship and, therefore, teaching, the name "sophist" seemed very apt to designate the new generation of men who around the year 450 became professionally engaged in a new field: the magistery of new ideas. Without being explicit, the word retained the concept implicit in *sophia* and its meaning denoted the concept of wielding and transmitting tastes or savors.

As previously indicated, this coincided with the "thinker's" emergence as a social figure to whom society reacted with hostility. The new name thus immediately acquired a pejorative connotation and likewise could not qualify as the stable name for the "thinker."

This brings us to the beginning of the fourth century. Plato is about to found his school near the Academy gymnasium. A school of what? Ten years following the death of Socrates the "thinker's" public position had improved somewhat, inasmuch as two generations of Athenians— understanding this to mean certain groups belonging to the upper classes—had already received the new education or *paideia*. Nevertheless, the hostility of the *demos* had not disappeared. Rather, the "thinkers" had become inured to its existence and they no longer behaved with the trusting nonchalance characteristic of their predecessors during the sixth century and the first half of the fifth. The style of "thought" thereafter became veiled, less spontaneous, and to a degree cautiously masked, so as not to bestir the religious faith of the multitude. The masses had reacted angrily to the "thinkers," not only because the latter were atheists, but because their mode of procedure seemed petulant and insolent. What name would a man like Plato, educated in Socratic irony, select for this profession and his message? The problem was complicated because the moment had arrived to cope with the confusion created amongst the Athenian populace by the utter divergence of intellectual disciplines. This augmented the urgency and the difficulty of arming oneself with a name that would be both defensive against public opinion and offensive against the other forms of "thought." We are speaking now of a people whose language is perhaps expressive of the greatest precision.

For a little over a century there had existed in the language a word whose meaning was extremely vague and noncommittal—the word *to philosophize*. It had been temporarily confined to a verb and an adjective. The adjective, I believe, first appeared in Heraclitus, although the term did not then have the meaning it was to acquire a century later.[12] Even by the final years of the fifth century it appeared in Thucydides, placed at a solemn juncture, upon Pericles' lips. It was paired with *philokalein* (a lover of beauty), another vague word, and the pairing prevailed for a long time. Both exclude the sense of professional practice. They convey, on the contrary, an informal manner of treating the arts, poetry, and ideas that were beginning to circulate among certain "elegant" Athenians around 450, the meaning of which had probably not altered since its not too distant birth.

The compounds that begin with φιλο (philo-) are very numerous in Greek. If we scan through them in an

12. It is a curious fragment, for it requires "philosophers" to know many things, whereas one of Heraclitus' most common battles is against "casuistry."

historical dictionary we see that most of them were formed in the last two-thirds of the fifth century and the first third of the fourth. Rarely does a particular morphological trend appear so pronouncedly in the nature of a fashion. For it is not popular words that are involved, and nearly all of them betray their "distinguished" origin. We must not, however, identify our attitude respecting these compounds with the prevailing attitude among the Greeks who coined and used them habitually. The tendency to use compound words is characteristic of the Greek language. This proclivity simultaneously inclines to the opposite and complementary phenomenon: a nation given to employing many compounds is generally unaware of their compound nature but rather of the ensuing unity wherein the compounds disappear. This becomes quite evident if we compare German, which is prone to compounds, with the Romance languages. We understand the compound precisely as a de-compound.

However, the instance of words beginning with φιλο, even within the context of compounds, represents something very special; for despite the fact that φιλο signified an independent word, it was transformed through overusage into something akin to a prefix. Thus its meaning of "a liking" or "a taste for" was almost totally obliterated and it retained only its frequentative, continuative sense, the suggestion of the quality or disposition, or propensity. In short, similar to the Latin suffixes *osus* and *bundus*.[13]

The foregoing is in reference to the verb *to philosophize* and its adjective, whose existence can be traced to around 500. With this in mind, let us turn to the appearance of the noun "philosophy," which is our prime interest, in the decade of 440.

Whoever examines all the positive and negative data

13. For some interesting observations on the compounds of φιλο, see Reith, *Grundbegriffe der stoischen Ethik*, pp. 24, 28, 29.

will recognize that it is not only unduly speculative to place the appearance of the name "philosophy" as a new and colorful expression among the coteries of "cultured" individuals, who when it emerged, more or less surrounded Pericles. Twenty years prior to this, Anaxagoras had arrived in Athens where the new breed of the "thinker" was as yet unknown. This unfamiliarity, plus the retiring life attributed to Anaxagoras, delayed the effects of his presence in the city, at least visibly. During those years only one disciple truly emerged: Archelaus —the first Athenian philosopher, whose disciple was Socrates. Meanwhile, however, the generation born fifteen years after Pericles was infected by the new ideas and felt great enthusiasm for the form of life introduced by peripheral Hellenic "thinkers." This induced men like Zeno, and perhaps Parmenides, Prodicus, and Protagoras to visit Athens and make brief appearances before elite circles. In this atmosphere the noun "philosophy" must have begun to circulate, signifying the pursuit of all the new disciplines, from natural philosophy to rhetoric. In conjunction with all this, medicine enjoyed a peculiar position.

Every word in a language is a usage formed within a segment of society and thereupon extended, sometimes to all of it. When one is dealing with a highly specialized social group, some of the words employed by it cease to be words of the language and are transformed into terms. Language is quite a different matter from terminology. A term is a word whose meaning is determined by a prior definition, and only by knowing the latter can one understand the former. Thus its meaning is precise. In language, however, a word conveys its meaning without prior definition. Hence it is always imprecise. Now then, the word "philosophy" did not originate as a term but as a normal word in a language and even as such its profile was exceedingly vague. Its conversion into a term can symbolize the history of Athenian intellectual life during the following half century.

This conversion occurred in Plato. His entire work is a dauntless attempt to render a rigorous meaning to the word "philosophy." His preoccupation with this name, however, dating from his earliest writing—that is, before he himself had a precise concept of the discipline he was later to refer to—is proof that his predilection for the word was something inherited from Socrates.

In Socrates the need to find a name to encompass his activity became increasingly acute and urgent. He was the first Athenian citizen to engage publicly in the new ideas, be it to expound or to criticize them. After Anaxagoras and Protagoras had been exiled, he unquestionably was clearly aware of the danger of his behavior. Nevertheless, no one was as intent as he upon distinguishing himself in people's minds from the naturalists and the rhetoricians. He was doubtlessly irritated to hear himself called, like the latter, a Sophist. The fact remains that fifty years later people were still calling him this. Was not "philosophy" the ideal word for his position? It was a soft name, diffuse in contour, inoffensive, and obviously anxious not to appear petulant. And yet for his message precisely, it offered the opportunity to convey a new meaning simply by employing the compound but de-compounding it, that is, underscoring its etymology. An attempt to pick out a name for something new within a language always prompts the seeker to pause abnormally before words, thereby isolating them almost as though they were words from a foreign tongue. Viewed through such abnormal optics—we have all had similar experiences—the etymology emerges from within the word as though its skeleton were emerging from its habitual body. Now, Socrates' message was remarkably paradoxical, for in contrast to the knowledge that was so ostentatiously flaunted in Athens in those times, the knowledge he claimed to possess was a "knowledge-that-does-not-know," *a docta ignorantia*. It is a formal refusal to be considered as σοφία *(sophos)* and even less as a master of various branches of knowledge, or as a Sophist. Precisely because his knowledge was negative, it was filled with a yearning for that which was lacking. By de-compounding the word, Socrates probably found the most exact expression for what he wishes to appear to be doing: striving, desiring to know. This in no way offered any positive step toward concretizing what constitutes the σοφία *(sophia)* of philosophy, but it delineated with great exactness his personal attitude. In this form, as a de-compound, the word ceased to be a word in the language. Its etymology defined it formally and furnished it with the hieraticism and asepticism that differentiated the "term" from the "word." In short, this kind of "juggling" performed upon the usual noun "philosophy" was one more ironic creation. Undoubtedly, the word, which like so many other compounds with φιλο-(philo-) was mannered to begin with, increased in its deviation. Irony, however, is clearly dissimulation. The Socratic schools are all stances oriented in different directions. Hence Plato's mannerism, at times intense, must have seemed even more striking, thus preventing him from ever being considered as an "Attic" writer. The "Asianism" forever imputed to him was simply mannerism. Hence it should not be surprising that possibly he is the author who employs the most compounds with φιλο-. They come to almost sixty!

This development makes us suspect that the illustrious discipline in all likelihood received its name primarily out of defensive reasons, as a precaution the "thinker" had to take against the wrath of his fellow-citizens who still clung to a religious position. Even in Socrates the etymological sense was able to reflect the negative knowledge he wished to impart, although in Plato it had already lost all connection with its intended content. The best proof of this is the conflict between Socrates and Plato for possession of the name to designate the divergent profession to which each was dedicated. The battle for this name proves two things: first, that by then the word was already imbued with a great attraction, and second, that its meaning in the language was extremely vague—in other words, the word barely denoted anything. Its meaning consisted rather in saying nothing precise, and in fact the only precise thing about it was its evasive meaning.

The name given to the philosophic profession would have been markedly different had it not been chosen with an eye to the "thinker's" social environment, but if the thinker with utter spontaneity had chosen a word to express as accurately as possible what was transpiring personally within himself as he was philosophizing—hence, a name of inner derivation. And in fact certain signs suggest that for a time it seemed as though the word ἀλήθεια (truth) might emerge as the name for philosophy. It was not confined, as Plato indicated, to Protagoras' principal work. Even more compelling is a certain discomfort to be noted in Aristotle regarding the noun "philosophy," thus impelling him to denominate "first philosophy" which he maintained constituted genuine philosophy. In actuality, when he wished to differentiate strictly between the mode of thinking that he brought to the science of principles—that is, to prototypal science—and wanted to isolate it from other modes of thought that had been pursued in Greece—poetry, Orphic cosmogonies and theologies, "natural science"—he named the line of the φιλοσοφήσαντες περὶ τῆς ἀληθείας (those who philosophized about truth).[14] This version, which is the usual one, makes no sense.

14. Met. 3, 983 b 3. He repeats it in 993 to 30.

Truth here does not mean any truth, but a type of radical, steadfast truth attainable only through a given mode of thought or a method. It designates simultaneously the result of the inquiry and the intellectual manner for attaining it. Now this was something ignored in ancient times. It had been initiated merely a few generations before, and hence in his *Protreptikos* he will speak more explicitly of "the science [φρόνησις] of that truth inaugurated by Anaxagoras and Parmenides."[15] Time and again in Aristotelian writing περὶ τῆς ἀληθείας (pertaining to truth) signifies properly the name of a science, to be precise philosophy in its strictest sense.

Although Aristotle believed that truth resides in judgments, this residing must be conceived of as a mere lodging, for truth essentially is not the truth of a judgment but the truth of beings themselves or the beings in *their* truth. Beings themselves do not appear in their truth, which does not necessarily imply that their mode of appearance constitutes the error. It is simply not "true." The truth of beings is inherently concealed and must be revealed; it has to be discovered. The same thing happened to the gods, though the latter revealed themselves of their own free will and there was no means to control the authenticity of their epiphany. Philosophy, in contrast, appeared as a methodical procedure for obtaining revelation—ἀλήθεια (truth). If one wishes to use the term "life experience" (*vivencia*) (*Erlebnis*), this methodical revelation was the underlying "*Erlebnis*" of the early philosophers, and ἀλήθεια was hence the name that from their own inwardness, corresponded to their profession.

Now a further radical distinction must be made between what philosophy is and what it is not if we are to comprehend how it originated and became differentiated not only from religion, but also from other modes of thinking.

15. Frag. 52.

That is, we must return to that moment when Parmenides began talking about something exceptionally strange, which he called "being." How and why did such a surprising adventure come about? People glibly repeat that philosophy is a questioning of Being. As if questioning oneself about such an irregular persona were the most natural thing in the world. This question must be examined a bit before one can talk about Being. It does not seem likely that this is what men who had lost faith in the gods and were discontent with φύσις (nature) should set out initially to seek. Perhaps Being at that time did not instigate the primordial question. Perhaps Being was an answer. When philosophy is said to be a questioning of Being, the premise is that it is going to try to discover the constitutive attributes of Being or of "beings." This implies however that one already has Being in front of him. How did it come to exist in men's minds? Does it not seem more likely that men, having lost the fundament of their lives, questioned themselves about some X phenomenon that would possess certain *prior* attributes—precisely the ones that justified the quest?